REPAIRING & MAINTAINING YARD EQUIPMENT & POWER TOOLS

REPAIRING & MAINTAINING YARD EQUIPMENT & POWER TOOLS

Mort Schultz

John Wiley & Sons, Inc.
New York • Chichester • Brisbane • Toronto • Singapore

This publication is designed to provide accurate and
authoritative information in regard to the subject
matter covered. It is sold with the understanding that
the publisher is not engaged in rendering legal, accounting,
or other professional services. If legal advice or other
expert assistance is required, the services of a competent
professional person should be sought. *From a Declaration
of Principles jointly adopted by a Committee of the
American Bar Association and a Committee of Publishers.*

Library of Congress Cataloging in Publication Data:

Schultz, Morton J.
    Repairing and maintaining yard equipment and power tools
/ Mort Schultz.
      p.   cm.
    Includes index.
    ISBN 0-471-53500-1 (cloth : acid-free paper). — ISBN
0-471-53501-X (paper)
    1. Power tools—Maintenance and repair. 2. Machinery—Maintenance
and repair. I. Title.
  TJ1195.S38   1994
  621.9—dc20   93-29808

Printed in the United States of America

10 9 8 7 6 5 4 3 2 1

The author acknowledges with gratitude the cooperation of Garden Way, manufacturers of Troy-Bilt equipment, for providing the outdoor power equipment used in illustrating the procedures described in this book.

Contents

PART TWO
SERVICING TWO-CYCLE ENGINES

PART THREE
REPAIRING OUTDOOR POWER MACHINES AND
ELECTRIC POWER TOOLS

Introduction to Outdoor Power Equipment

Outdoor power machines can be classified into four categories:

1. Those you push,

2. Those you sit on,

3. Those you hold in your hand or strap to your back, and

4. Those that remain stationary.

The machines that you push include lawn mowers, snowthrowers, garden tillers, and sickle bar mowers. One example is shown in Figure I.1.

Outdoor power machines you sit on are accelerated, steered, and braked similarly to the way you drive a car (Figure I.2). They are called riding mowers by some and lawn tractors by others.

FIGURE I.1.   The sickle bar mower is one of the newest types of power machines. The unit is used to clear a path through underbrush.

Outdoor power machines you hold in your hands or strap to your back are generally lightweight machines, such as chain saws, grass trimmers, and grass/leaf blowers.

Outdoor power units that do their work while remaining stationary include generators and shredders (Figure I.3).

Outdoor power machines are outfitted with one-cylinder internal combustion engines that either use gasoline or a mixture of gasoline and motor oil as the fuel or are powered by electric motors. The number of outdoor power machines with electric motors are insignificant compared to those powered by gasoline or motor oil mixtures.

There are two types of one-cylinder internal combustion engines—the four-stroke or four-cycle engine and the two-stroke or two-cycle engine. The terms "stroke" and "cycle" mean the same thing. Four-stroke engines use gasoline as fuel. Two-cycle engines require a mixture of gasoline and motor oil as fuel.

FIGURE I.2.   A lawn tractor possesses a steering wheel, an accelerator, and brake pedals.

Whether the equipment you own has a four- or two-cycle engine, it's possible to keep that engine in use for your lifetime by mastering the disciplines of maintenance, troubleshooting, and repair.

Maintenance refers to services that are needed to keep an engine running flawlessly and to prevent the onset of problems that will occur if the equipment is deprived of these services.

Troubleshooting is the term describing inspections and tests that lead to the identification of the cause of an engine problem. Most engine problems have a number of possible causes. For example, a four-cycle engine that is hard to start has more than a half dozen potential causes. Some are centered in the fuel system, others in the ignition system, and still others inside the cylinder, sometimes called the combustion chamber.

FIGURE I.3.   Stationary shredders are equipped with one-cylinder four-stroke engines as are power mowers, tillers, lawn tractors, and most all other outdoor power machines.

Troubleshooting allows you to pinpoint or isolate the troublesome area. Once the cause of the problem is found, the repair can be made.

The maintenance, troubleshooting, and repair tasks described in this book are graded as to difficulty. One * means that the task can be done by someone who has little or no do-it-yourself experience. Two ** indicate tasks that require some previous experience. Three *** mark projects that advanced do-it-yourselfers will feel comfortable about tackling.

PART ONE

Maintaining, Troubleshooting, and Repairing One-Cylinder Four-Stroke Engines

1

What You Should Know about Four-Stroke Engine Operation

The job of the one-cylinder four-stroke internal combustion engine is to provide power (Figure 1.1). It does this by getting a piston, which is inside the combustion chamber, to move up and down or from side to side at a rapid rate of speed.

The piston turns the crankshaft. The job of the crankshaft is to turn another part. In the case of a walk-behind or riding mower, that part is the blade that cuts grass. With a snowthrower, the crankshaft turns a rubber paddle or an auger that scoops snow off a driveway or sidewalk. An auger of different design on a garden tiller churns up earth in preparation for planting a garden.

With a four-cycle engine, it takes four strokes of the piston to complete one power

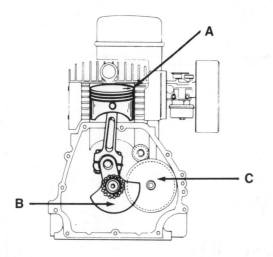

FIGURE 1.1.   Internal parts of a one-cylinder four-stroke internal combustion engine are (A) the piston, (B) the crankshaft, and (C) the camshaft.

cycle of the crankshaft. The four strokes are intake, compression, power, and exhaust.

THE INTAKE STROKE

During the intake stroke (Figure 1.2), gasoline flows into the combustion chamber through an intake port. The intake port is open because an intake valve has been lifted off the port by a cam that is part of the camshaft. There is another cam on the camshaft that controls an exhaust valve. Each cam is shaped like an egg.

The camshaft is turned by the crankshaft. As the crankshaft turns the camshaft, the cam that controls the intake valve pushes

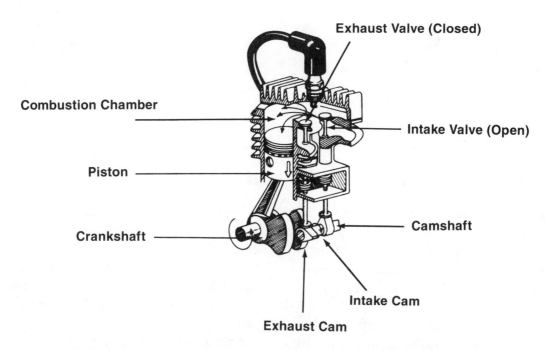

FIGURE 1.2.   The intake stroke of a one-cylinder four-cycle engine.

against the valve stem, forcing the valve off the intake port. With the intake port open, gasoline is able to flow into the combustion chamber from the fuel system.

The other player in this scenario is the piston. During the intake stroke, it is swooping down inside the combustion chamber. This swooping action produces a low pressure area (or vacuum) in the space left vacant above the piston. Gasoline is thus able to flow from an area of higher pressure, which is inside a carburetor, into an area of lower pressure, which is inside the combustion chamber.

THE COMPRESSION STROKE

During the compression stroke (Figure 1.3), which follows the intake stroke, the piston is on the rise from the bottom of the combustion chamber. The camshaft has rotated to a position that brings the cam past the intake

valve, releasing pressure on the valve stem and allowing the valve to seal the intake port. Since the exhaust port is also closed, the combustion chamber is sealed.

The compression stroke gets its name from the compression of gasoline to a fraction of its original volume by the piston as it rises in the cylinder. In most one-cylinder four-stroke engines, gasoline is compressed to one-sixth of its original volume. This is necessary if gasoline is to ignite and burn to release energy. Uncompressed gasoline in a sealed cylinder will not ignite.

THE POWER STROKE

As the piston reaches the top of the combustion chamber, the spark plug fires and ignites the compressed gasoline, which begins to burn rapidly—almost explosively, in fact (Figure 1.4). The ensuing flame spreads from the tip of the spark plug to the

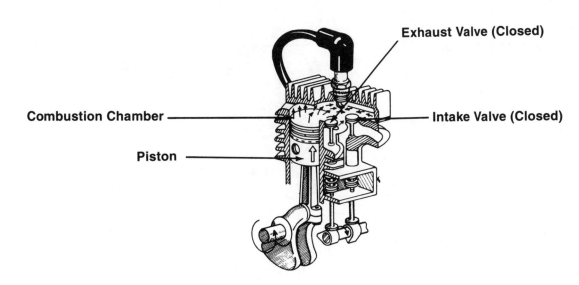

Exhaust Valve (Closed)

Combustion Chamber

Intake Valve (Closed)

Piston

FIGURE 1.3. The compression stroke of a one-cylinder four-cycle engine.

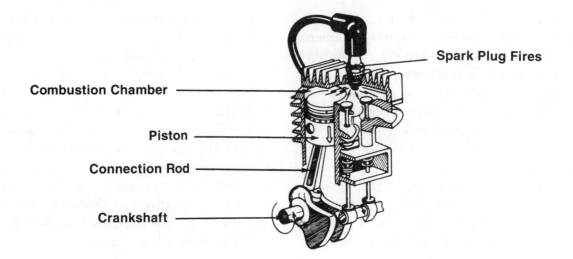

FIGURE 1.4.   The power stroke of a one-cylinder four-cycle engine.

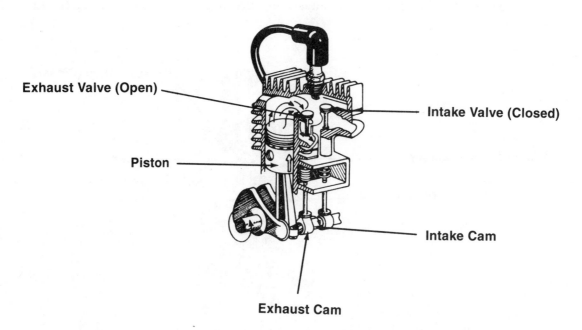

FIGURE 1.5.   The exhaust stroke of a one-cylinder four-cycle engine.

far reaches of the combustion chamber. As gasoline burns, gases are released that expand and push against the piston to shove the piston down with tremendous force. When this happens, a rod connecting the piston to the crankshaft causes the crankshaft to turn, which drives the blade or auger of the outdoor power machine.

THE EXHAUST STROKE

Once gases expend their energy, they become waste products (or exhaust). If they were to remain inside the engine, they would contribute to the production of acid, carbon, and sludge which are harmful to engine parts. So they have to be expelled. Here's how that happens.

The piston once again swoops down to the bottom of the cylinder. As it starts moving upward, the piston pushes the exhaust toward the exhaust port, which is now open, because the cam has pushed against the exhaust valve stem to lift the valve off the exhaust port (Figure 1.5). The piston pushes the waste gases out the exhaust port into the atmosphere.

Now the process starts over again—intake, compression, power, and exhaust. It is this sequence of events that provides you with power for your tools.

2

Maintaining a
Four-Stroke Engine
to Prevent Damage

There are two reasons for doing maintenance on a regularly scheduled basis:

1. To prevent damage to the engine.
2. To keep the engine operating at optimum efficiency.

In this chapter, maintenance services that are necessary to prevent damage to a one-cylinder four-stroke engine are described. They include (1) selecting the correct gasoline for the engine, (2) changing oil, and (3) keeping the engine clean so it won't overheat. In Chapter 3, maintenance services necessary for keeping an engine running at optimum efficiency are described.

NOTE
Every project in this chapter is either a one * or two ** task. One * projects are those that do-it-yourselfers with little or no experience should be able to handle. Two ** projects are those that can be done by do-it-yourselfers who have some experience.

CHOOSING GASOLINE*

Choosing the correct gasoline for a one-cylinder four-stroke engine is easy enough. Follow these recommendations:

- Use regular unleaded gasoline that has an 87 or 88 octane rating. Gasoline having a higher octane rating may cause engine damage.

- You can use gasoline containing no more than 10 percent ethyl alcohol (also called ethanol or grain alcohol) as long as that gasoline, which is referred to as gasohol, has an 87 or 88 octane rating.

- Don't use gasoline that contains methyl alcohol (also called methanol or wood alcohol). Methyl alcohol will eat away rubber and plastic parts of the fuel system. It can also result in poor engine performance when the equipment is used under low ambient temperature conditions.

- Don't pour any additive into the fuel tank with gasoline unless the additive is specifically recommended by the manufacturer in the owner's manual. An unauthorized additive can damage the engine.

FILLING THE FUEL TANK*

You may not think that filling the fuel tank of a one-cylinder four-stroke engine is a big deal, but if you make a mistake that introduces dirt into the fuel system, you could end up having to dismantle the fuel system to overhaul the carburetor. Careless filling of the fuel tank can also cause serious personal injury. Therefore, follow these recommendations:

- Buy a can that is specifically designed for transporting gasoline to haul fuel for your engine. You can get one from a dealer of automotive parts and supplies.

- Do not store gasoline in the can. After 30 days, stored gasoline can turn gummy. Besides, stored gasoline is a fire hazard. If you have any gasoline left over after filling the fuel tank of a one-cylinder four-stroke engine, pour it into the fuel tank of your car.

- Use a clean funnel to pour gasoline from the can into the fuel tank of your four-stroke engine. If you have washed the funnel, make sure it is dry. Introducing drops of water into the fuel system will result in an engine-starting problem.

CAUTION
Gasoline presents health and safety hazards. Avoid inhaling fumes. Fill the fuel tank outdoors so there is ample ventilation. Do not smoke or bring a flame or anything that may create a spark near the equipment.

• After filling the fuel tank, wipe off the fuel tank cap before screwing it on the tank in case it picked up dirt from the surface on which you laid it.

SELECTING THE BEST MOTOR OIL*

The oil recommended in the owner's manual for your engine may not be the most effective to use in terms of protecting the engine.

Improvements in motor oil technology occur on the order of once every 10 years, with the last change occurring in 1989. You may, therefore, want to consider the following information the next time you buy oil for your engine:

• The most advanced motor oil is identified by the letters "API SG," which are printed on the label of the container in which the oil comes (Figure 2.1). API stands for

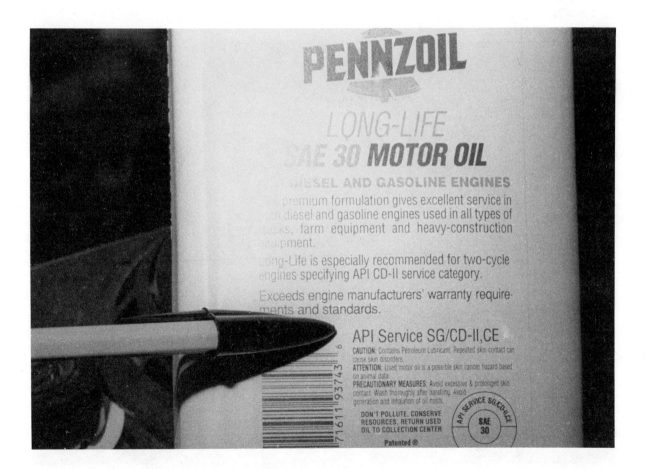

FIGURE 2.1.   The best oil for the engine of your outdoor power machine is one designated by the symbol "API Service SG." Disregard other symbols used in conjunction with this, such as "CD-II, CE," which indicate that the oil is suitable for use in diesel engines.

American Petroleum Institute. The "S" of SG stands for *s*park-ignition system. The "G" of SG means that the oil possesses the most advanced additives to protect the engine. Before SG, SF oil was the one to use. Therefore, regardless of what the owner's manual recommends, use oil designated by the letters API SG.

• Use your owner's manual to select the weight (viscosity) of oil that meets the ambient temperature conditions anticipated for your region during the time that the equipment will be in use. The viscosity is printed on the label of the container. If you've misplaced the owner's manual and an ambient temperature above freezing (32°F or 0°C) will prevail for most or all of the time that the equipment will be in use, select an oil viscosity designated by the symbol "SAE 10W-30" or "SAE-30" (Figure 2.2). SAE stands for Society of Automotive Engineers. If an ambient

FIGURE 2.2. Use SAE 30 or SAE 10W-30 oil if the prevailing ambient temperature is 32 degrees F or higher.

temperature below freezing will prevail for most or all of the time that the equipment will be in use, select an oil designated by the symbol "SAE 5W-30."

CAUTION

Do not use SAE 10W-40 or SAE 20W-50. It can harm the engine.

NOTE

The maintenance schedule printed in the owner's manual for your outdoor power machine probably recommends that you change the oil every 15 or 25 hours that the equipment is used. Whatever it recommends for you to do, do.

FIGURE 2.3. Whenever you do any work on the engine, disconnect the spark plug cable from the spark plug and point the end of the cable away from the terminal of the plug.

CHANGING MOTOR OIL**

Haphazardly changing the oil of a one-cylinder four-stroke engine can result in engine damage, injury to the person doing the oil change, unnecessary work, and harm to the environment. Since you don't need any of this, here are the steps that should be followed:

1. Start the engine and let it run for about 10 minutes to get the oil hot. When hot, oil becomes more fluid and will flow more readily from the engine.

2. After 10 minutes, turn off the engine, disconnect the spark plug, and point the end of the cable away from the spark plug (Figure 2.3).

3. Check the owner's manual to find the location of the oil drain plug. If the manual has been misplaced, look for the plug on the bottom or side of the engine. If the plug is under the engine, place a pan

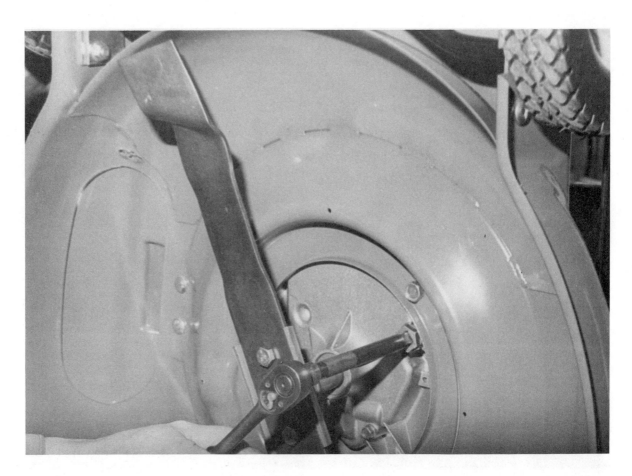

FIGURE 2.4. If the oil drain plug is under the engine, remove the drain plug and quickly place a receptacle beneath the drain hole to prevent oil from running down the machine onto the ground.

beneath it and unscrew the plug to let the oil drain from the engine (Figure 2.4).

If the oil drain plug is on the side of the engine and the hole doesn't have a drain tube (Figure 2.5), fashion a drain trough from a piece of flexible metal such as aluminum (Figure 2.6). The trough allows oil to flow from the engine in a straight path, keeping it from running over the outside of the engine and onto the ground. You may have to tip the engine to get all of the oil drained out of it.

Be patient. Wait for oil to drain completely. Complete drainage is attained when you don't see another drop dripping from the engine for 60 seconds.

4. Carefully pour the contaminated oil from the pan into a receptacle that has a cap— for example, an empty fruit juice jar. Do not allow oil to pour on the ground and don't pour it down a toilet or sink drain. This stuff is toxic and harmful to the environment. Dispose of it by taking the

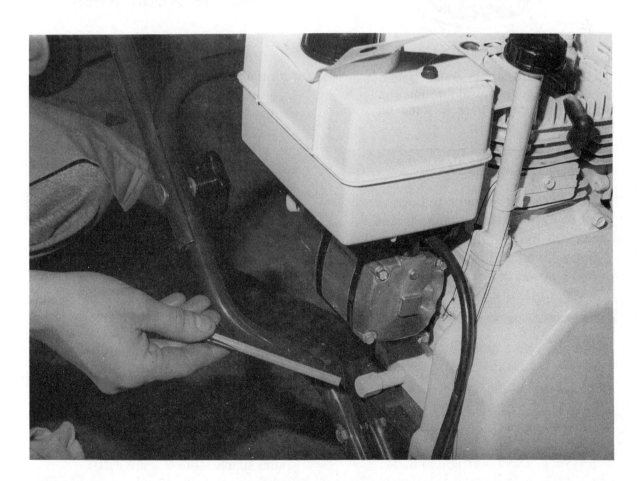

FIGURE 2.5. The manufacturers of some engines with the oil drain on the side of the engine equip the drain hole with a tube.

FIGURE 2.6. **If a side-mounted drain doesn't have a tube, make a drain trough similar to the one illustrated here to keep oil from pouring on the ground.**

CAUTION
Oil may be hot enough to burn you, so be careful. Researchers suspect that oil may, under certain conditions, be a carcinogen. Be safe and wear gloves. If any oil gets on you, wash it off with soap and water.

receptacle to a municipal waste site or a service station that accepts used oil.

5. Screw the oil drain plug back into place by hand. Be careful not to cross threads. When you can't turn the drain plug with your fingers, turn it with a wrench until it is snug. *Don't* overtighten it.

6. Insert a clean funnel in the oil fill tube or hole. Pour in fresh oil until the oil level reaches the FULL mark on the oil dipstick or the notch inside the fill hole indicating that the engine is filled.

7. Connect the spark plug cable to the spark plug, start the engine, and let it run for one minute. Then shut the engine off, disconnect the spark plug cable, and check around the oil drain plug to see if there is any oil, indicating a leak. If you find oil, tighten the oil drain plug a little at a time until no more oil leaks out.

CLEANING THE CYLINDER HEAD**

One-cylinder four-stroke engines like those on outdoor power equipment rely on air circulating around the cylinder head to carry away heat and keep the engine from overheating. Dirt and grass clippings may get packed between the fins of the cylinder head (Figure 2.7). If this happens and the engine runs hotter than it should, serious damage can result. It may require you to overhaul the engine. To keep this from happening, clean between the fins every time you change the oil, as follows:

1. Disconnect the spark plug cable and point its end away from the plug.

2. Remove the engine cover so you can get at all parts of the cylinder head—not just the fins that are exposed (Figures 2.8 and 2.9).

3. Sweep debris from between the fins with a brush or use a can of compressed air. You can purchase clean, compressed air in a photography supply store or in a computer supply store (Figure 2.10).

4. Replace the cover and reconnect the spark plug cable.

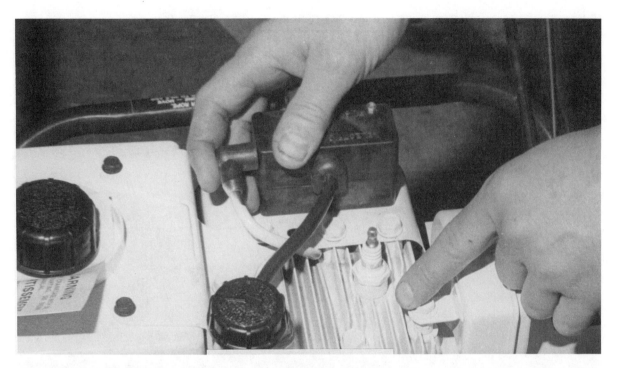

FIGURE 2.7. The fins of the cylinder head must be kept clean if the engine is to be cooled properly. Excess heat will damage an engine.

FIGURE 2.8. To get at all the fins of the cylinder head of this machine, you have to remove a cover. To do that, you first have to take off other parts.

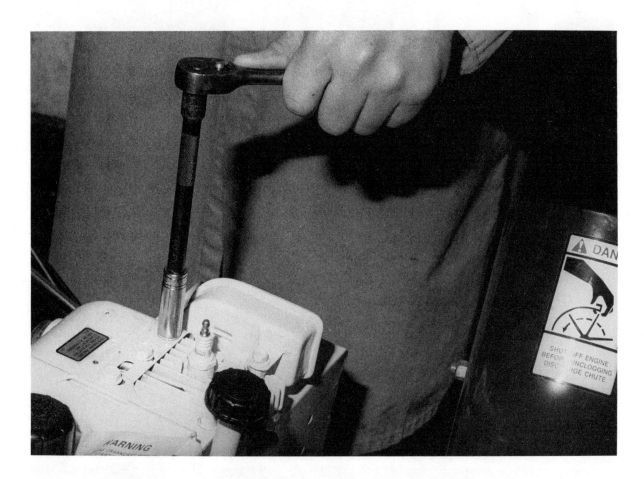

FIGURE 2.9. **As you take off bolts, label which bolt goes into which hole.**

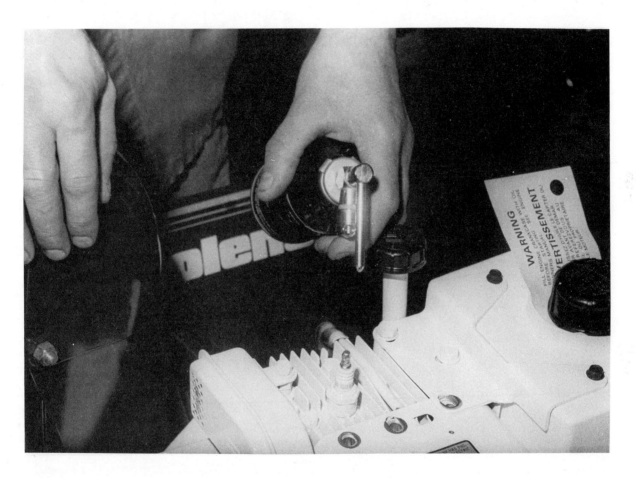

FIGURE 2.10.   A can of compressed air is useful for this and other jobs you'll be doing on the engines of your outdoor power equipment. Compressed air is available from photographic or computer supply stores.

3

Maintaining, Testing, and Adjusting Your Four-Stroke Engine for Optimum Performance

The maintenance procedures necessary to keep a one-cylinder four-stroke engine running smoothly involve servicing the ignition and fuel systems, preparing the engine for storage during the off-season, and purging the engine of carbon. Purging the engine of carbon, which is sometimes called a power tune-up, is discussed in Chapter 4.

A flaw in performance makes itself known in one of the following ways:

- The engine won't start.
- The engine starts, often only after extended cranking, and stalls.
- The engine misses and may then stall when a load is imposed. Missing is characterized

by uneven running when, for example, you attempt to plow through snow or mow a lawn. Although the engine may stall, it will start again when the load is relieved.

- The engine lacks power. When you put the engine under load, there is a noticeable reduction in power.
- The engine surges. Surging is characterized by an alternate increase and decrease in speed, as if the engine can't make up its mind.

A performance problem can be caused by a lack of maintenance or by damage that requires repair. Maintenance is comparatively easy to do. Except for the power tune-up discussed in Chapter 4, none of the procedures should take you longer than 30 minutes. On the other hand, repairing the engine to resolve a problem will usually require overhauling the ignition system, fuel system, or the engine itself. Therefore, when a flaw in performance occurs, do the maintenance services outlined in this chapter, followed by a power tune-up if the circumstances outlined in Chapter 4 apply, before tackling a repair.

All tasks described in this chapter are graded with one * which means that novice do-it-yourselfers should find them within their range of ability, or two ** which means that some experience would be helpful.

THE IGNITION SYSTEM

The ignition system of a one-cylinder four-stroke engine consists of a spark plug and components that produce and deliver current needed by the plug to make sparks (Figure 3.1). If the spark plug can't make sparks,

gasoline in the combustion chamber won't ignite and the engine won't start. If the firing end (electrodes) of the plug is fouled or if the plug is damaged, the engine might start, depending on the extent of the fouling or damage, but will then miss and/or stall.

There is a preliminary step to take before delving deeper into the ignition system if you have trouble starting the engine. Press the terminal end of the cable onto the spark plug in case the cable has loosened (Figure 3.2). Crank the engine to see if the problem has been solved. If the problem remains, go on to the next step.

The Spark Plug*

The spark plug causes more problems with one-cylinder four-stroke engines than any other component. Here is what to do about it:

1. Disconnect the spark plug cable and point it away from the spark plug.
2. Using a socket wrench that fits the spark plug, turn the plug counterclockwise to unscrew it from the engine (Figure 3.3).
3. Notice whether the plug has a gasket. If it does, discard the gasket (Figure 3.4).
4. Inspect the plug for a crack in the porcelain. Replace a damaged plug (see steps 7 through 13).
5. Examine the firing (electrode) end of the plug. Are the electrodes worn? Replace the plug.

   Are the electrodes coated with carbon or oil? Do they appear burned (eroded)?

Spark Plug

FIGURE 3.1. The spark plug of a one-cylinder engine is placed either on top of the engine as with a garden tiller or on the side of the engine. If the spark plug is on top, the piston in the engine moves up and down (vertically). If the spark plug is on the side, the piston moves from side to side (horizontally).

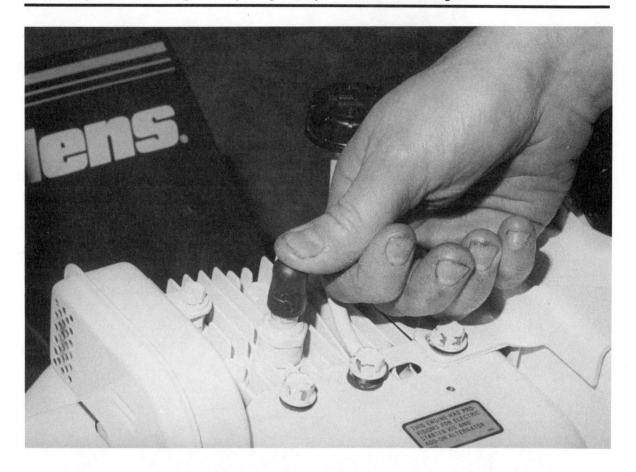

FIGURE 3.2.   A loose spark plug cable could keep the engine from starting or make it hard to start.

Carbon means that the engine has been running on an overly rich fuel mixture. Check to see if the air filter is dirty (see page 46) and replace the plug.

Oil on electrodes indicates major damage to the engine. Piston rings are probably worn and the engine has to be overhauled (see Chapter 12).

Eroded electrodes, which have a ghostly white appearance, mean that the engine is overheating. Change oil, if

applicable, and clean the cylinder head (see Chapter 2). Perhaps a power tune-up is also needed to reduce the temperature at which the engine is running (see Chapter 4). Replace the plug.

6. If the spark plug isn't damaged, worn, or fouled, use a small wire brush to clean the electrodes. If the plug had a gasket, buy a new gasket and place it around the shoulder. Then, check the spacing (gap) between the electrodes

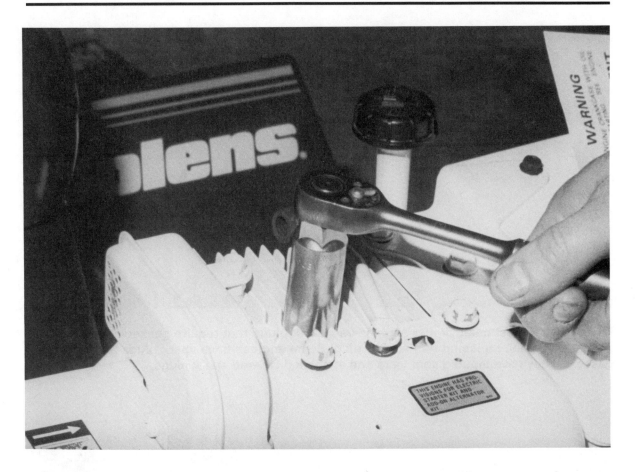

FIGURE 3.3. The socket you use to remove and install spark plugs should fit the plug. If there is too much space between the socket and the six-sided part of the plug shell, the plug may be damaged.

with a feeler gauge and reinstall the plug as described in steps 7 through 13.

Replace the Spark Plug*

7. If you have to install a new spark plug, make sure the new plug is the right one for your engine (Figure 3.5). Also see to it that the plug comes with a new gasket if it is designed to have a gasket. Buy a spark plug electrode gauge if you don't already own one.

8. Look in the owner's manual for the gap (space) to set between the electrodes. This gap, for example, 0.030, 0.045, 0.060 inch, varies from engine to engine. If you have misplaced the owner's manual, ask a dealer who sells your make of outdoor power equipment to look it up for you.

9. Select the feeler of the gauge that corresponds to the recommended electrode gap setting. Insert the feeler between the electrodes and move it back and

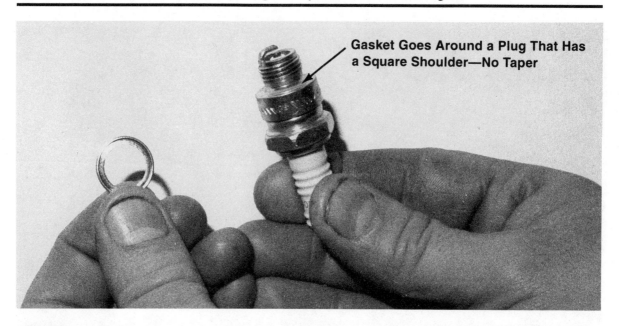

Gasket Goes Around a Plug That Has a Square Shoulder—No Taper

FIGURE 3.4. Most one-cylinder engines use spark plugs that require gaskets. Always use a new gasket when replacing this kind of plug. Some engines have spark plugs that don't use gaskets. They have tapered shoulders and are called tapered spark plugs.

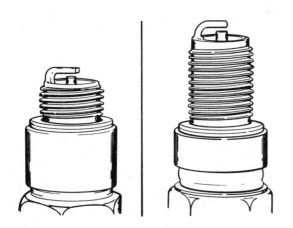

FIGURE 3.5. Spark plugs differ as to length. Make sure you buy the correct plug for your engine as spelled out in the owner's manual. If you use a wrong plug, the engine won't run right.

forth (Figure 3.6). The gap is set correctly if you feel slight resistance.

10. If the gap is too tight or too loose, make the adjustment by bending the movable (side) electrode. The only tool you should use is the notched tang which is part of the spark plug electrode gauge (Figure 3.7). Using any other tool—pliers, for example—will result in damage that may ruin the plug. Remember, too, that you set the electrode gap by bending the *side* electrode—never the electrode extending down through the center of the spark plug. Bending this center electrode will kill the plug. In bending the side electrode, move it a little at a time to open or close the gap. Then use the feeler to see if you have hit the correct spacing.

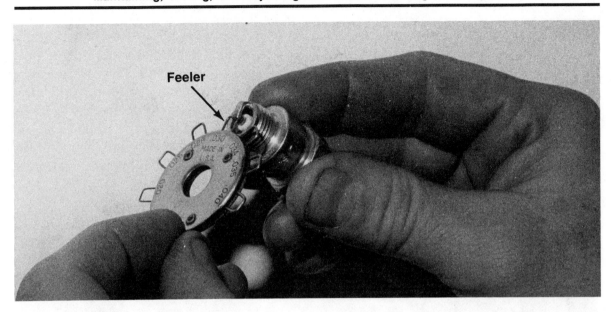

FIGURE 3.6. Move the feeler back and forth between the electrodes to determine if the space (gap) between the electrodes is set correctly.

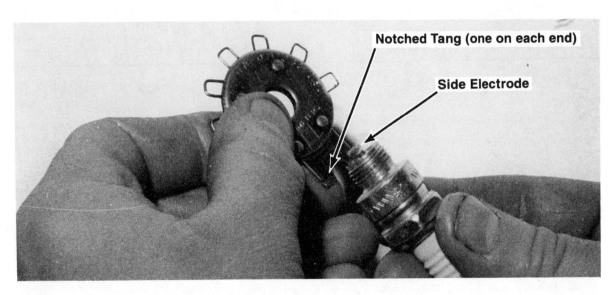

FIGURE 3.7. If you have to set the gap between electrodes, bend only the side electrode using the notched tang which is part of the spark plug feeler gauge.

11. When the electrode setting is to specification, use a thread cleaner to clean the threads of the spark plug port in the cylinder head (Figure 3.8). You can buy a thread cleaner from the dealer who sells you the plug.

12. If the spark plug comes with a gasket, see that the gasket is in place around the shoulder of the plug. Screw the plug into the cylinder head by hand until you can no longer turn it. Then, using a socket wrench that fits the plug, turn the plug a half turn more if the plug uses a gasket. If the plug doesn't use a gasket, turn it a quarter turn. Be careful not to cross the threads or overtighten the plug. If you do, you will have trouble getting the plug out of the cylinder head again, and you could even damage the engine.

13. Connect the cable to the plug and try starting the engine to determine if you

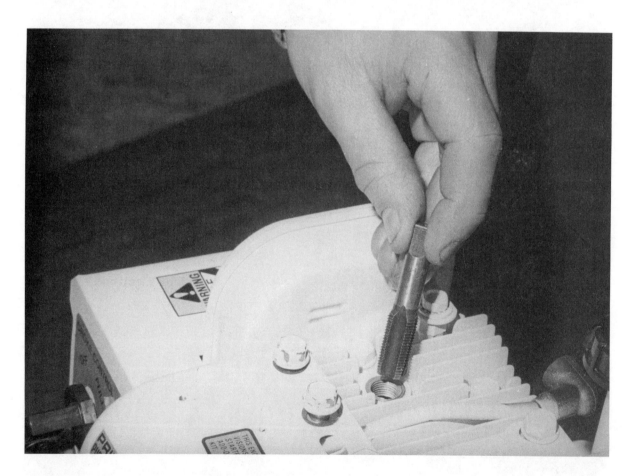

FIGURE 3.8. Insert the thread cleaner into the spark plug port and turn it to clean grit and oil off the threads. Grit and oil can interfere with the installation of the plug or cause it to seize in the cylinder head.

have gotten rid of the engine performance flaw. If the problem is still present, test the rest of the ignition system.

The Spark Intensity**

The spark intensity test, which is done with a tool called a spark intensity tester that looks like a hockey puck, establishes whether the ignition system is delivering voltage to the spark plug. Converging in the center of the tool are the tips of two or three screws that penetrate through the side of the puck. If the spark intensity tester you purchase has three screws, use any two.

The spark intensity tester is available from an outdoor power equipment dealer. In addition to the tester, you will need an alligator clip if one isn't already attached to the tester. The cost of this equipment is reasonable. Here is what to do:

FIGURE 3.9. The spark intensity tester is attached to the spark plug cable and cylinder head bolt.

1. If the alligator clip is not part of the tester, attach one of its jaws to one of the screws of the spark intensity tester.

2. Disconnect the spark plug cable from the spark plug.

3. Shove the spark plug cable onto the end of a screw of the spark intensity tester. Make sure the metal terminal of the cable is in contact with the screw.

4. Attach the other jaw of the alligator clip to a cylinder head bolt.

The setup should appear as illustrated in Figure 3.9. Now, crank the engine by pulling the rewind starter rope a few times, watching the tips of the screws that converge in the center of the spark intensity tester as you do (Figure 3.10). If the ignition system is delivering electricity to the spark plug, you will see a bright blue spark shooting between the tips of the screws. If there isn't any spark or the spark is yellow or orange, there is an ignition system malfunction that has to be repaired as described in Chapter 9.

FIGURE 3.10. Pull the rewind starter several times as if you were starting the engine. Lack of a blue spark shooting between the screws in the center of the tester identifies the cause of a problem as an ignition system failure.

NOTE

If you have trouble distinguishing the color of the spark jumping between the tips of the screws, cover one hole of the spark intensity tester with black electrician's tape. This will make the spark more distinguishable.

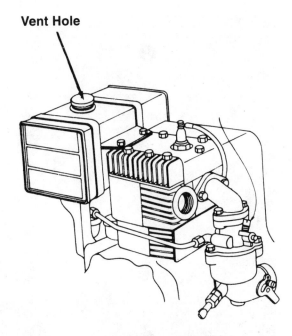

Vent Hole

FIGURE 3.11. Look for a vent hole on the outside and inside of the fuel tank cap.

THE FUEL SYSTEM

If an engine starts, the engine is getting fuel. If the engine is hard to start or starts promptly but lacks power, misses, stalls, or surges, the following maintenance procedures done in the order of presentation may resolve the problem.

The Fuel Cap Vent*

Take the cap off the fuel tank and check both sides of it for a small vent hole (Figure 3.11). If a hole is present and it's plugged with dirt, pressure that builds up in the fuel system can't bleed off and will upset the balance of the fuel system, curtailing the quantity of gasoline that should flow to the engine. This will make the engine hard to start or cause another flaw in performance.

Using a strand of wire that is smaller in size than the diameter of the hole so you don't enlarge the hole, gently poke at the dirt to loosen it. Then, blow it away with a burst of compressed air (Figure 3.12). If you don't have an air compressor, buy compressed air in a can from a dealer of photo-

graphic or computer supplies. Determine if the starting problem has been eliminated.

The Air Filter*

There is a filter inside the housing of a one-cylinder four-stroke engine that filters dust from the air that is scooped in by the engine to mix with gasoline. Pure gasoline in a combustion chamber won't ignite unless it is mixed with air.

If the air filter clogs, the amount of air entering the engine will be curtailed and the engine will be forced to operate on an overly rich fuel mixture. This can lead to hard starting or another flaw in performance.

Most one-cylinder four-cycle engines of outdoor power machines use a paper or poly-

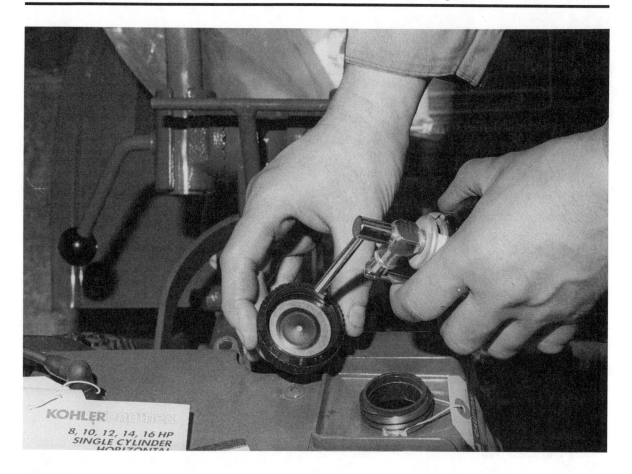

FIGURE 3.12. Use compressed air in a can to clear away dirt that may be plugging the vent hole.

urethane air filter. Some have a polyurethane filter in combination with a replaceable screen. Others have a paper filter wrapped in a polyurethane filter. To service the air filter of your engine, open the air filter housing by unscrewing the cover or releasing the clips holding the cover. Then, do this:

For a Paper Filter

1. Take the filter out of the housing (Figures 3.13 and 3.14). As you do, notice whether the seal around the perimeter of

NOTE

Although it is recommended that a paper air filter be replaced once a year, it may have to be changed more often if outdoor power equipment is used frequently. You can find out if a new filter is needed by taking the old filter from the housing and holding it up to the light. If it looks dirty, replace it.

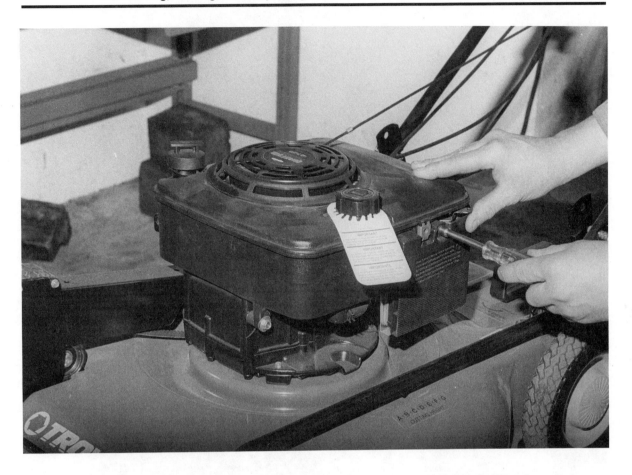

FIGURE 3.13.   To remove the air filter, take off the cover over the air filter housing.

the filter is facing in or out. The seal of the new filter has to face in the same direction to keep dirt from flowing around the edges of the filter and entering the engine (Figure 3.15). Dust that gets inside an engine may cause damage.

2. Buy a new filter from a dealer who sells the make of outdoor power machine you own. Use a clean rag to wipe the inside of the filter housing and also the cover. Place the filter in the housing and reattach the cover.

For a Polyurethane Filter

1. Take the filter out of the housing.
2. Wash the filter in a mixture of liquid dishwashing detergent and warm water, squeezing the filter until no dirt comes out of it.
3. Rinse the filter in clean water.
4. Put the filter on paper towels and squeeze it to remove excess water.

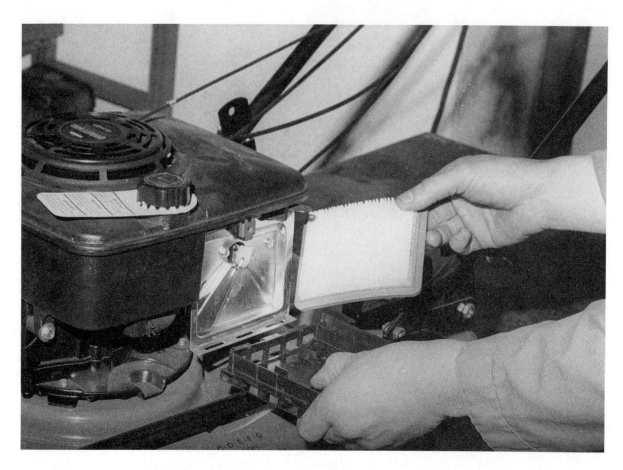

FIGURE 3.14.   The simplest air filter is made of paper.

FIGURE 3.15.   When you install a new filter, be sure it's put into the housing correctly—in this case, with the seal facing in.

CAUTION
Do not twist the filter. You will tear it.

NOTE
A polyurethane filter should be cleaned and oiled every three months that the outdoor power machine is operated.

5. Spread a little SAE 30 motor oil over one side of the filter. Turn the filter over and spread a little oil on the other side. Put on rubber gloves and press down on the filter to distribute the oil as evenly as possible.

6. Wipe out the filter housing and cover, and install the filter.

For a Combination Polyurethane Filter and Screen

1. Inspect the filter housing after removing the filter. If there is a mesh-type element

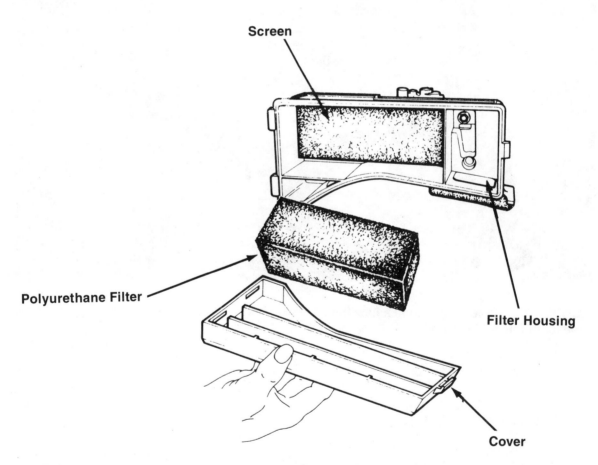

Screen

Polyurethane Filter

Filter Housing

Cover

FIGURE 3.16.   Some engines use a polyurethane air filter combined with a screen.

(screen) behind where the filter has been positioned, you can service the polyurethane filter as we described earlier (Figure 3.16).

2. Remove the screen. You will probably have to unscrew the filter housing from the engine to get at the clips holding the screen.

3. Install a new screen, clean out the housing, and reinstall the filter. Screens are available from a dealer who sells your make of outdoor power machine.

NOTE
A combination polyurethane filter and screen should be serviced every three months that the outdoor power machine is operated.

For a Paper Filter Wrapped Inside a Polyurethane Filter

This filter is referred to as a dual-stage air filter. If the polyurethane wrapper is kept clean

FIGURE 3.17. Someone removing the air filter housing cover of this machine may think that the unit is serviced only with a polyurethane filter.

and oiled (see earlier discussion) you may never have to replace the paper filter (Figures 3.17 and 3.18). The paper filter is a backup in case the polyurethane filter clogs. If the paper filter gets dirty, replace it.

Engine Speed*

If servicing the air filter doesn't correct a performance problem, examine the carburetor for external screws by which to set the speed of the engine when it is idling and when it is under a load (Figure 3.19). The owner's manual or a dealer who sells your make of outdoor power equipment can tell you if there are idle speed and load adjustment screws on the carburetor. If there are, do this:

CAUTION
When making adjustments with the engine running, keep your hands away from any revolving part. Engage the adjustment screw with a screwdriver and not your fingers.

FIGURE 3.18.   When the polyurethane filter is removed for cleaning, the paper filter is exposed.

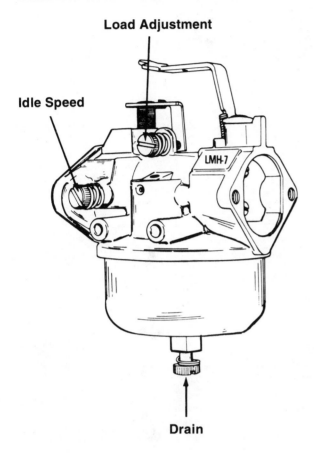

Load Adjustment

Idle Speed

LMH-7

Drain

FIGURE 3.19. The number and arrangement of the various screws on a carburetor varies from carburetor to carburetor. This particular carburetor has three screws. Consult the owner's manual for the setup in the carburetor of your outdoor power machine.

1. If the engine misses and/or stalls while idling, with the engine off turn the idle speed adjustment screw clockwise until it just touches bottom. Do not ram the screw down. Then, turn the screw counterclockwise 1 turn, start the engine. Does it now run without missing and/or stalling? If it doesn't, turn the screw clockwise $1/8$ of a turn and test perfor-mance again (Figure 3.20). Keep doing this until the problem clears up or it becomes obvious that missing and/or stalling is being caused by some other malfunction.

2. If the problem is that the engine misses and/or stalls only when a load is imposed on the outdoor power machine, start the engine and turn the load adjustment screw clockwise or counterclockwise $1/8$ of a turn. Then, put a load on the engine by running the machine over grass, through snow, or whatever use the equipment is designed for. Judge whether the miss is better or worse to determine how the screw should be manipulated. Then turn it in that direction $1/8$ turn at a time until performance gets better, or it becomes obvious that the problem is not being caused by a misadjusted load adjustment screw.

NOTE

Other fuel system problems and repairs are described in Chapter 6.

ENGINE STORAGE**

The reason for doing the following services prior to putting outdoor power equipment away for the season is to prevent an engine performance problem when the machine is put back into use:

1. Change the oil and clean the cylinder head (see Chapter 2).
2. Service the air filter (see pages 46–52).

FIGURE 3.20. Turn carburetor adjustment screws slowly, stopping when the engine runs at optimum performance.

3. Add a fuel stabilizer or drain gasoline from the fuel tank and carburetor. If one or the other isn't done, gum deposits and varnish that form in gasoline can clog the fuel system passages in the carburetor, restricting the delivery of gasoline to the engine when you again run the engine. This will cause poor performance.

Fuel stabilizers are available from auto parts and supply dealers or outdoor power machine dealers. If the machine is going to be kept in storage for a year or longer, it is better to drain the gasoline. This is done in several ways. The following method can be used if a draining device as illustrated in Figures 3.21 and 3.22 is not available:

Remove the fuel tank cap and use a syringe with a long stem to siphon gasoline from the tank, or start the engine and let

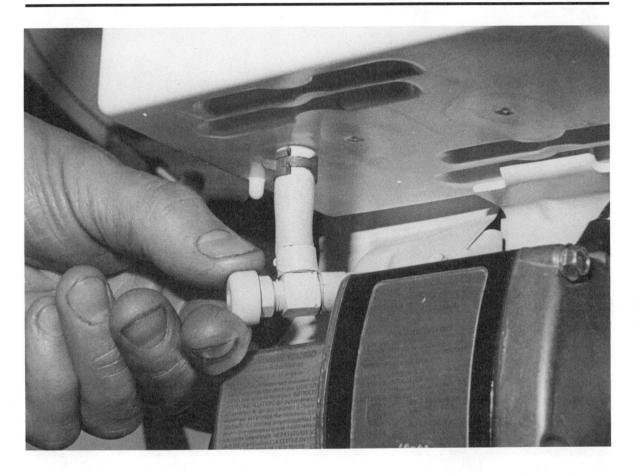

FIGURE 3.21. This machine has a shut-off valve that is closed to stop gasoline from flowing between the fuel tank and carburetor. To drain the fuel tank, start by closing the valve.

---

it run until it is out of gas. If you use the siphoning approach, deposit the gasoline into a receptacle that has a cap so you can take it to a waste site for disposal. Don't dump it on the ground, down a drain, or into the fuel tank of your car.

To drain gasoline from the carburetor fuel bowl, press the drain valve or remove the drain plug in the bottom of the bowl

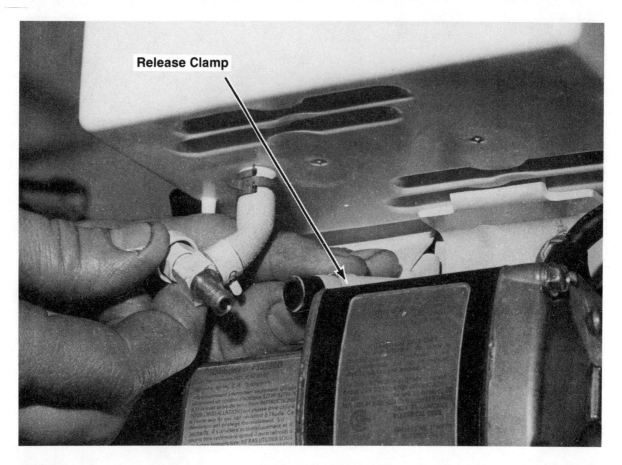

Release Clamp

FIGURE 3.22. Release the clamp that holds the valve to the fuel line going to the carburetor. Pull the valve out of the line and hold the end over a receptacle. Then, open the valve to let gasoline drain.

(Figures 3.23 and 3.24). If the carburetor bowl doesn't have a drain plug or drain valve, disconnect the fuel line at the carburetor and hold the open end of it in the receptacle to let gasoline drain.

4. If the spark plug hasn't been serviced in some time, do that now (see pages 36–38).

5. Remove the spark plug and pour one ounce of SAE 30 oil (Figure 3.25) into the engine through the spark plug port in the cylinder head. Install the spark plug and slowly pull the rewind starter rope out all the way. Do this twice to distribute the oil along the walls of the combustion chamber and around the piston. The oil will help protect these parts from rust during the storage period.

FIGURE 3.23.   This carburetor has two screws in the bowl. One is for adjustment; the other, which is being pointed to, is a drain valve that's pressed to drain off gasoline. If your carburetor has this kind of setup, press one screw and then the other to determine which one is the valve.

FIGURE 3.24.   This carburetor has two plugs in the bowl. If your carburetor has this kind of setup, remove one plug and then the other to determine which is the drain plug.

FIGURE 3.25. To protect the inside of the engine during the storage period, pour or squirt an ounce of SAE 30 oil into the spark plug port. An ounce is three squirts with an oil can.

4

Restoring
Engine Power

The one-cylinder engine of an outdoor power machine can lose 30 percent or more of its maximum power after only 100 hours of operation. This has a deleterious effect on the performance of the outdoor power machine and may cause the owner to discard a machine that can be easily restored with a power tune-up.

"Power tune-up" is the term used to describe the purging of carbon from the cylinder head, piston, and valves of an engine. In addition to restoring power, the removal of

61

carbon reduces the temperature at which an engine operates. As carbon builds up, engine temperature will rise. If it rises high enough, the engine will suffer severe damage. Therefore, a power tune-up should be done if the engine is overheating (see Chapter 8).

The way to determine whether an engine is overheating is to shut it off after it has been run for 15 minutes. Slowly bring your hand toward the cylinder head without touching it. If heat becomes too intense, causing you to draw your hand away, the engine is overheating.

POWER TUNE-UP: PRELIMINARY STEPS

To do a power tune-up, you will need a torque wrench, which is a relatively inexpensive instrument that you can purchase from a dealer of automotive parts and supplies or from an outdoor power equipment dealer. The torque wrench is equipped with a gauge that will measure whether you are tightening (torquing) cylinder head bolts to specification. If you leave bolts too loose when you reattach the cylinder head, the engine will

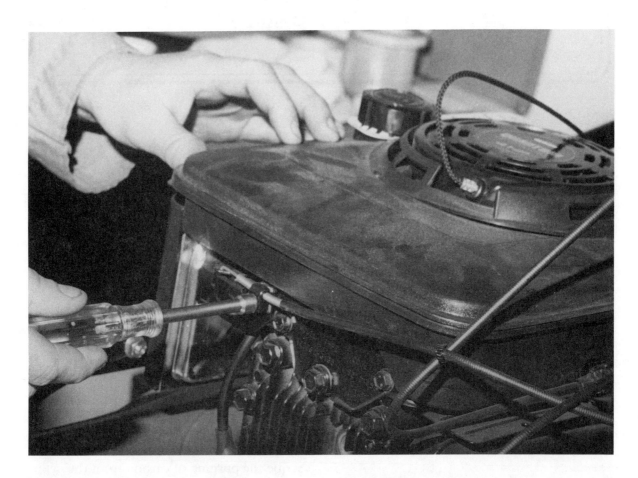

FIGURE 4.1. To remove the cylinder head, you will probably have to take off a cover that is blocking it. Here, for instance, we start by releasing cables attached to the cover.

lose compression. Loss of compression will result in faulty performance. On the other hand, if you overtighten the cylinder head bolts, you will probably crack the cylinder head. It will then have to be replaced—an expensive proposition.

There are two types of torque wrenches. One type measures torque in foot-pounds (ft.-lbs.). The other type measures torque in inch-pounds (in.-lbs.). The wrench you need for doing a power tune-up is one that measures torque in foot-pounds.

THE POWER TUNE-UP

Here's how to give your engine a power tune-up:

1. Take the cable off the spark plug and remove the spark plug from the cylinder head.
2. If the cylinder head is blocked by a cover, remove the cover (Figures 4.1, 4.2, and 4.3).
3. Start with any cylinder head bolt and proceed clockwise around the cylinder

FIGURE 4.2.   Remove bolts holding the cover to the machine.

FIGURE 4.3. **If the cover doesn't come off after all visible bolts are removed, look for hidden bolts.**

head to remove all the head bolts (Figure 4.4). As you take out each bolt, identify it to the hole from which you have taken it. One way to do this is to put a piece of masking tape on the bolt and near the hole. Write a number—1 for the first bolt and hole, 2 for the second, 3 for the third, and so forth—on each piece of tape identifying a bolt. Write the same number on the piece of tape identifying the bolt hole. Each bolt should be returned to the hole from which it came.

4. When all the bolts have been taken out, pull off the cylinder head (Figure 4.5). If it won't come off, do not bang it with a hammer and do not pry it off with a screwdriver. You will ruin the head. Tap it with a wood or rubber mallet a few times before trying again. Continue in this way until the head comes off.

5. Discard the cylinder head gasket. If pieces of gasket stick to the head or to the mounting surface, scrape them off with a plastic or wood scraper. The head and mounting surface of the engine

FIGURE 4.4.   As you remove each head bolt, identify it and the hole from which you take it.

against which the gasket rests must be clean to prevent a loss of compression (Figure 4.6).

6. Use a wire brush to clean carbon from the inside of the head (Figure 4.7). When this has been done, check the head for warpage by holding a straight-edge across the back side of the head and seeing if you can squeeze a 0.003-inch ruler or feeler between the head and straightedge (Figure 4.8). Do this in four different spots across the head. If you can get the feeler in the space be-

tween the straightedge and head at any spot, take the part to a machine shop and have it resurfaced on a lathe. If the technician at the machine shop says a lot of metal had to be taken off to get the head true, use two gaskets when you re-install the head. The extra head gasket will take up the volume and help prevent the loss of compression that usually results by shaving away too much metal.

7. After servicing the cylinder head, turn your attention to the piston and valves (Figure 4.9). Look inside the combus-

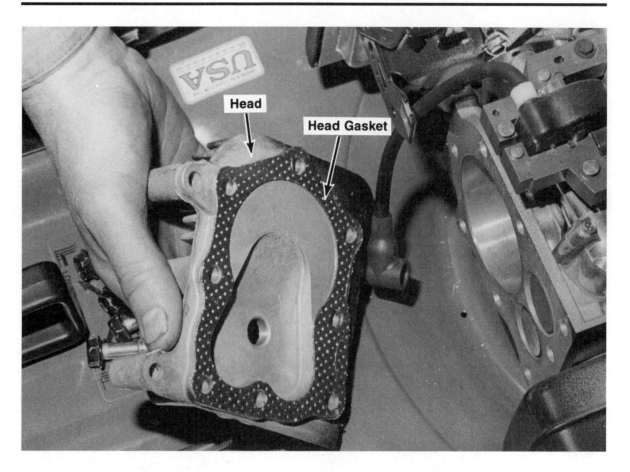

FIGURE 4.5.   Remove the cylinder head and its gasket.

tion chamber to determine where the crown (top) of the piston is positioned. If it is not at top dead center in the chamber, turn the working end of the outdoor power machine (blade or auger) by hand until the piston crown comes up to that position. Turning the flywheel will also rotate the crankshaft to get the piston and valves positioned so they can be cleaned.

8. Using a wooden implement, copper penny, or brass washer, scrape carbon from the piston crown and from the tops of the valves (Figure 4.10). Don't use any other instrument to do this. You might damage the piston and valves.

9. Blow loose carbon out of the combustion chamber with compressed air. If you don't have an air compressor, buy a can of compressed air from a dealer of photography or computer supplies.

10. When carbon has been removed, turn the working end of the outdoor power

FIGURE 4.6. Clean the mounting surface to give the head gasket a firm surface against which to seat, thereby preventing a loss of compression.

machine by hand to lower the piston in the combustion chamber. Put a new gasket on the cylinder head and position the head against the engine, making certain that the gasket doesn't slip (Figure 4.11). Insert bolts and tighten them by hand.

11. Before tightening bolts with the torque wrench, determine whether the engine is aluminum or cast iron by holding a magnet to the cylinder head (Figure 4.12). A magnet won't be attracted to aluminum. It will be attracted to cast iron.

12. Using the torque wrench, tighten bolts to the applicable specification, as follows:
    • If the cylinder head is aluminum and the engine is rated at five or less horsepower, tighten head bolts to 12 ft.-lbs. If the cylinder head is aluminum and the engine is rated at over

FIGURE 4.7. Clean carbon from the head, using a wire brush if necessary.

five horsepower, tighten head bolts to 15 ft.-lbs.

- If the cylinder head is cast iron and the engine is rated at five or less horsepower, tighten head bolts to 15 ft.-lbs. If the cylinder head is cast iron and the engine is rated at over five horsepower, tighten head bolts to 18 ft.-lbs.

  Tighten bolts in a cross-cross pattern in three equal stages. For example, with an aluminum engine rated at five or less horsepower, tighten each bolt 3 ft.-lbs. Then, go back and tighten each of them another 3 ft.-lbs. Finally, go back and tighten them all another 3 ft.-lbs.

13. After you have run the engine the first time following a power tune-up, turn it off and let it cool down. Then, use your torque wrench to retighten bolts to specification, thereby making certain that each head bolt is still at the correct torque.

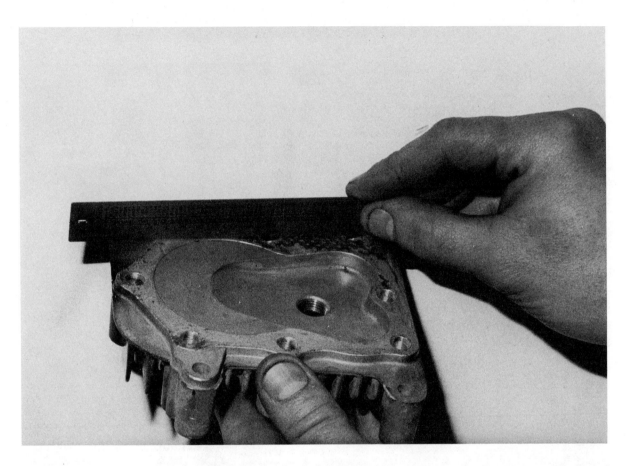

FIGURE 4.8.   If there is any space between the straightedge and cylinder head, have the head resurfaced at a machine shop.

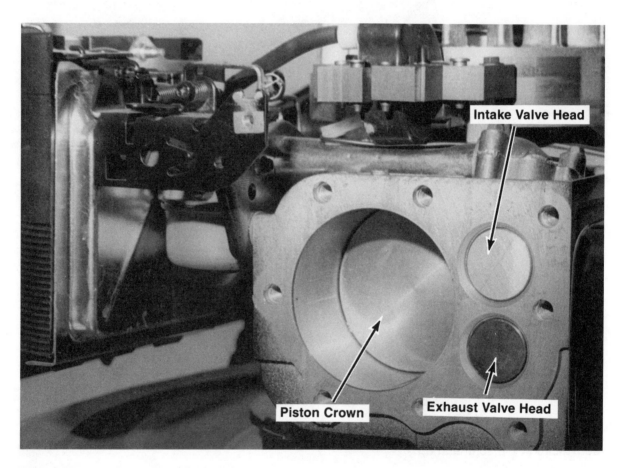

FIGURE 4.9. The ultimate purpose of this service is to clean carbon from the crown of the piston and the heads of the valves, which will restore full power to the engine.

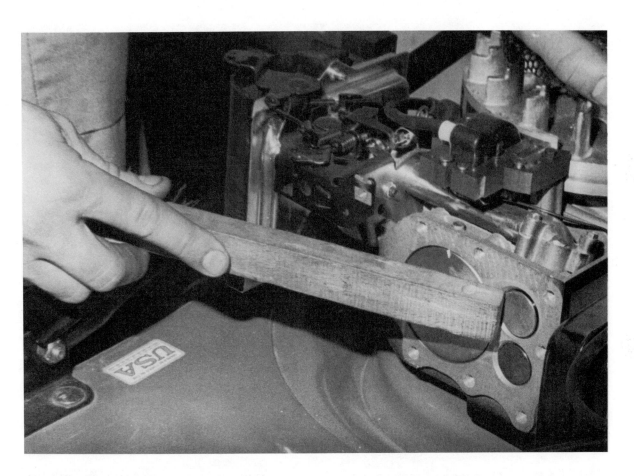

FIGURE 4.10.   Scrape off carbon with a wooden implement, copper penny, or brass washer.

FIGURE 4.11.   Whenever you remove the cylinder head, use a new gasket when you put the head back on the engine.

FIGURE 4.12.   Use a torque wrench to tighten the cylinder head bolts.

5

An Introduction to Troubleshooting and Repairing a Four-Stroke Engine

The three chapters which follow—Chapters 6 through 8—discuss the problems most likely to affect the performance of a one-cylinder four-stroke engine. The information will permit you to identify and repair what is causing one of the following engine problems:

- Failure to start
- Hard starting

- Missing and stalling when a load is imposed on the engine
- Lack of power
- Surging
- Excessive vibration
- Knocking
- Consuming or leaking motor oil
- Overheating.

Each chapter begins with a chart listing the possible reasons for the problem. Charts are arranged so you can proceed from the easiest to the most difficult repair that may have to be made.

Use each chart as a guide. Beginning with the first cause listed in the chart, note whether an entry next to it tells you if the condition has been discussed in a previous chapter. If it has been, turn to that chapter. If it hasn't, the explanation of how to troubleshoot, if an explanation is necessary, is given in the chapter following the chart. Once you have ruled out this first cause as the reason for the problem, go on to the next cause and so on until you find out why your engine isn't operating properly.

When it comes to the repair, the cause given in the chart may suggest the repair.

For example, no gasoline in the fuel tank as being the reason why the engine won't start would obviously suggest that you fill the tank.

If the repair procedure is relatively easy to do, but requires some explanation, that explanation follows the troubleshooting procedure described in the chapter. An example of this kind of repair is getting rid of a tank of gasoline that has been contaminated with water.

Finally, if the repair is complicated or difficult, it is handled in a separate chapter. Falling into this category are revamping the ignition system, overhauling the fuel system, repairing the starting system, and rebuilding the engine.

6

Troubleshooting and Repairing Starting Problems

An engine needs three things to start: fuel, a spark to ignite fuel, and adequate force (compression) to compress fuel so it can ignite and expel maximum energy. If one of the three is missing or lacking in quantity, the engine won't start or will be hard to start. Although an engine that won't start and an engine that is hard to start are two different problems, they are both discussed in this chapter because most of the causes are common to both.

Guide to Troubleshooting & Repairing an Engine Starting Problem

Possible Cause	What to Do	Refer to
No gasoline in fuel tank (engine won't start)	Fill the tank	—
Obstructed fuel cap vent	Open the fuel cap vent	Chapter 3, page 45
Closed fuel shut-off valve (engine won't start)	Open the fuel shut-off valve	This chapter, pages 78–79
Clogged carburetor (engine won't start)	Test for a restricted carburetor	This chapter, page 79
Choke is sticking (hard starting)	Clean the choke	This chapter, pages 79–81
Gasoline is contaminated	Drain contaminated gasoline	This chapter, pages 81–84
Engine is flooded	Service the air filter; clear a flooded engine	Chapter 3, pages 45–52; this chapter, pages 84–85
Fouled or damaged spark plug	Service the spark plug	Chapter 3, pages 36–39
Breakdown in the ignition system	Troubleshoot the spark plug cable and adjust ignition timing	This chapter, pages 85–86
Lack of compression	Test compression	This chapter, pages 88–89
Inoperative starting system	Pinpoint starter failure	This chapter, page 89
Damaged flywheel key	Replace the flywheel key	This chapter, pages 90–95

REMINDER

The following procedures are graded with one *, two **, or three ***. One * indicates a project that can be done by novice do-it-yourselfers. Two ** signify projects that can be done by do-it-yourselfers having some experience. Three *** are projects best handled by an advanced do-it-yourselfer.

THE FUEL SHUT-OFF VALVE*

Many four-stroke engines of outdoor power machines have a fuel shut-off valve on the carburetor or on the fuel line to the engine. You or someone else may have closed the valve to do a service procedure and forgotten to open it. A closed shut-off valve keeps gasoline from reaching the engine. Consequently, the engine won't start.

If you don't know whether your engine is equipped with a fuel shut-off valve, examine the carburetor and fuel line for a spigot-type device that you can turn or refer to the owner's manual. If your machine has a fuel shut-off valve, the owner's manual will reveal where it is located. As a last resort, you can ask a dealer who sells your make of outdoor power equipment to point out the shut-off valve.

RESTRICTED CARBURETOR TEST

If little or no gasoline is present in the combustion chamber because of a restriction in the carburetor, the engine won't start.

Troubleshooting*

Follow these steps:

1. Disconnect the spark plug cable from the spark plug, and face the terminal end of the cable away from the spark plug.

2. Pull the rewind starter rope five times.

3. Remove the spark plug from the cylinder head and feel the electrode end of the plug. If it is dry, gasoline is not getting into the combustion chamber. See Chapter 10 for the procedures that are necessary to make repairs.

THE CHOKE

The carburetors of most outdoor power machine engines are equipped with a manually operated choke that closes over the throat of the carburetor when a richer fuel mixture is needed to start a cold engine. With most machines, the choke is controlled by a cable that extends from the handlebar of the equipment to a plate or a slide mechanism. If your engine has a choke plate, it lies in the upper part of the carburetor throat. If the engine has a slide mechanism, it is positioned on the side of the carburetor (Figure 6.1). If the choke plate or slide mechanism gets stuck in the open or closed position, the engine when cold will be hard to start or it may start but will stall.

NOTE
Before turning your attention to the choke, make sure you are operating the device according to the engine starting instructions in your owner's manual.

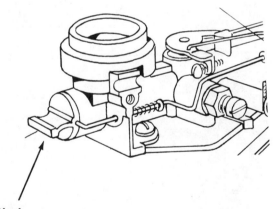

Choke

FIGURE 6.1. This carburetor is equipped with a slide-type choke that allows the operator to provide a richer fuel mixture for starting a cold engine.

*Troubleshooting**

Follow these steps:

1. Disconnect the spark plug cable from the spark plug and point the terminal end of the cable away from the spark plug.
2. Uncover the carburetor.
3. Move the choke cable to close and open the choke plate or slide mechanism as an assistant observes the functioning of the

device. It should move freely from a fully closed to a fully open position.

*Repair***

Spray around the pivot points of a choke plate with choke and carburetor cleaner and wipe dirt from the choke cable. Then, operate the choke a few times. If the choke is a slide mechanism, pull out the slide and apply a few drops of choke and carburetor cleaner to the slide. Wipe dirt from the choke cable

FIGURE 6.2. To remove the fuel tank, begin by taking the cover off of the flywheel housing. Although the procedure varies somewhat from engine to engine, you can be guided by what you see here.

and manipulate the slide mechanism by means of the cable several times.

CONTAMINATED GASOLINE

Hard starting or lack of starting will occur if moisture or particles of dirt have mixed with gasoline. Moisture is often the result of condensation that develops in the engine. Dirt can be introduced into the fuel tank with gasoline from the gas can that is used to transport it. Particles in fuel can also result if the engine fuel tank is metal and is rusting.

Troubleshooting*

Follow these steps:

1. Disconnect the cable from the spark plug and point the end of it away from the spark plug.
2. Remove the fuel tank cap.

FIGURE 6.3. Remove the bolts that hold the fuel tank to the engine.

3. Draw some gasoline into a clean, dry syringe and deposit it into a clean, dry glass receptacle.

4. Let the sample sit for 15 minutes before inspecting the gasoline by looking through the glass. If there is water in the gasoline, the two will have separated with a clear-cut demarcation line between them. If particles are present in gasoline, they will be floating around in the liquid or will have fallen to the bottom of the glass.

Repair **

Follow these steps:

1. With the spark plug cable still disconnected, use a syringe to draw all the gasoline from the fuel tank. Deposit the volatile fluid into a receptacle that will be discarded, such as a fruit juice jar which has a cap. Screw caps on the fuel tank cap and discard receptacle.

2. If the fuel tank is positioned above the carburetor, place a pan or rags under the

FIGURE 6.4.   Lift off the tank and release the fuel line.

fuel line to absorb gasoline that may drip. Then, release the clamp holding the fuel line to the fuel tank and pull the line off.

3. Undo the bolts holding the fuel tank to the engine and take the tank off (Figures 6.2–6.4).

4. When the fuel tank is free, take off its cap and pour any gasoline remaining in the tank into the discard receptacle.

5. If the problem is condensation in the gasoline, fill the tank halfway with rubbing alcohol, screw on its cap, and slosh the alcohol around in the tank. Then, un-screw the cap, pour alcohol into the discard receptacle, and screw the fuel tank back on the engine.

Now, drain gasoline from the carburetor bowl if you can. Look for a draining device in the bottom of the bowl (Figure 6.5). If you find a hex-shaped plug, loosen it with a wrench. Place a pan under the bowl, remove the plug by hand, and let gasoline drain. Reinstall and tighten the plug, and pour gasoline from the pan into the discard receptacle.

If the device in the bottom of the carburetor bowl is a slotted screw that has a

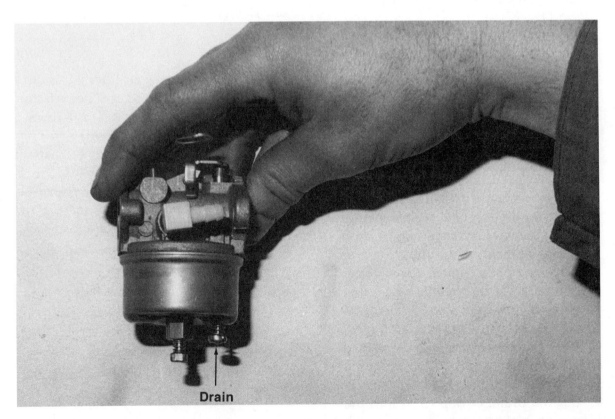

Drain

FIGURE 6.5. The carburetors of most one-cylinder four-cycle engines have a draining device in the bottom of the carburetor bowl.

spring around it, proceed cautiously. This may be a carburetor adjusting screw so don't turn it. Place a pan under the screw and press it in with a screwdriver. If the device is a drain, gasoline will come out. Some carburetors have two screws in the bottom of the bowl—a drain screw and an adjusting screw. Usually, the drain screw is the smaller of the two. After draining the bowl, pour gasoline from the pan into the discard receptacle.

If the drain mechanism in the bottom of the carburetor bowl is a petcock, hold a pan under it and turn the petcock counterclockwise until no more gasoline drips from the opening. Close the petcock and pour gasoline from the pan into the discard receptacle.

6. If the problem is rust particles being deposited in the gasoline from a metal tank that is rusting, install a new tank.

7. Fill the fuel tank with gasoline.

CAUTION

Working around gasoline is dangerous. Do not smoke or bring anything that may produce a spark near the equipment. Work outdoors and try not to inhale fumes. Wear rubber gloves. Wash thoroughly if gasoline gets on your skin. Take the receptacle containing contaminated gasoline to a toxic waste site or to a gas station for disposition. Do not dump the fluid on the ground, pour it down a drain, or deposit it into the gas tank of your car.

FLOODED ENGINE

One-cylinder four-cycle engines need a precise fuel mixture to start promptly and run flawlessly. The fuel mixture consists mainly of air and some gasoline. If the mixture has an excessive amount of gasoline, the engine will flood and may not start. If it does start, it will stall or run poorly. A dirty air cleaner will cut off air, which leads to flooding, but the most common cause is a tendency by the operator to keep the choke plate closed over the carburetor throat for much too long a time.

Troubleshooting*

You will usually smell gasoline when the engine floods.

Repair*

Inspect and service the air filter if it is dirty (see Chapter 3). If the filter is not a factor, purge the engine of excess fuel, as follows:

1. With the choke plate or slide mechanism wide open, close the fuel shut-off valve. If the engine doesn't have a fuel shut-off valve, but it has a fuel line, squeeze the fuel line shut with a pair of vise grip pliers.

2. Pull the rewind starter rope until the engine starts.

3. Let the engine run until it stalls.

4. Open the fuel shut-off valve or reattach the fuel line.

5. Start the engine, following instructions for starting outlined in the owner's manual.

An engine will also flood if the choke sticks in the closed position (see page 80) or if a carburetor float system isn't operating properly (see Chapter 10).

IGNITION FAILURE

An ignition failure that can keep the engine from starting or that makes the engine hard to start is often the fault of a worn or damaged spark plug (see Chapter 3). Once this has been discounted, look for other ignition system problems by using a spark intensity tester to find out whether the ignition system is producing adequate voltage (see Chapter 3). If the test reveals that there is an ignition system malfunction, turn to Chapter 9 where overhaul of that system is discussed. The only other problems with an ignition system that can affect the delivery of voltage to the spark plug is a damaged cable, through which voltage is transmitted from the voltage-creating components to the spark plug, and faulty ignition timing.

Troubleshoot the Spark Plug Cable*

The insulation that surrounds the cable which delivers voltage to the spark plug may

FIGURE 6.6. The engine cover has to be removed to inspect this spark plug cable.

be cracked. Like water, electricity takes the path of least resistance, which is through the crack in the cable to a metal part of the engine along which the cable extends. If the spark plug isn't getting any voltage, the engine will refuse to start. If some voltage is getting through, the engine may be hard to start and will probably miss and/or stall once it does start.

1. Disconnect the cable from the spark plug.
2. Beginning at the spark plug end of the cable, proceed up the cable and examine

the insulation for cracks. Bend the cable back and forth as you do to uncover any crack in the insulation that may not be visible by making a cursory inspection (Figures 6.6 and 6.7).

Replacing a cracked spark plug cable involves replacing the ignition coil (see Chapter 9).

Adjust Ignition Timing***

An outdoor power machine engine is equipped with one of two kinds of ignition

Ignition Coil

FIGURE 6.7. Notice how close the cable is to the engine. If the cable cracks at this point, current needed by the spark plug cannot reach the plug and the engine won't start.

systems. The modern version is an electronic or solid-state system. The other type is a magneto system, which is also referred to as breaker point or contact point ignition.

Magneto ignition was in use long before solid-state ignition was adopted, so there are still millions of outdoor power machines in operation that have it. The normal wear incurred by the breaker points of magneto ignition results in changes in ignition timing. Ignition timing, also called spark timing, refers to the instant that spark is delivered to the combustion chamber by the spark plug to ignite the fuel mixture. Periodic adjustment of timing is necessary to prevent hard starting and/or lack of power.

Readjusting ignition timing of an engine equipped with solid-state components is not necessary. A solid-state ignition system doesn't have moving parts. The spark timing of a solid-state system is set at the factory when the engine is manufactured and doesn't deviate. Magneto ignition, however, is another matter. Although service manuals provide a detailed procedure for timing a magneto ignition system, that procedure requires using a special gauge to show the position of the piston relative to top dead center. The following method doesn't require this gauge.

1. Disconnect the spark plug cable and remove the spark plug.
2. Remove the flywheel (see below).
3. Using a feeler gauge of a size corresponding to the breaker point gap specification, adjust the spacing (gap) between the movable and stationary breaker points. With some engines, this is done by means of an adjusting screw that

---

NOTE

To set ignition timing, you need the recommended breaker point gap specification for your engine. The breaker points of practically all outdoor power machines with magneto ignition are adjusted to 0.020 inch, but you should check with a dealer who sells your make of engine to determine whether this holds true in your case.

---

brings the movable point closer to or further away from the stationary point. With other engines, it is done by loosening a bolt that secures a clamp around the condenser. The stationary point is positioned on the end of the condenser. Therefore, sliding the condenser will bring the stationary point closer to or further away from the movable point (Figure 6.8).

NOTE

If contact points are burned or pitted, or cannot be adjusted, replace them and the condenser (see Chapter 9).

---

4. Insert a wood dowel into the spark plug hole until it touches the top of the piston. Then, turn the crankshaft by hand until the piston is at the highest point (top dead center) in the combustion chamber. You can determine when this position has been reached by the movement of the dowel.

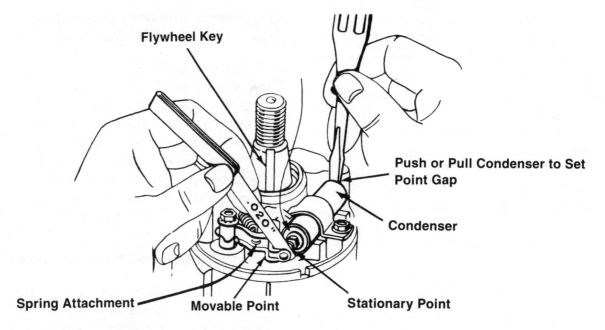

FIGURE 6.8. Setting breaker points involves moving the stationary point seen here as part of the condenser closer to or further away from the spring-loaded movable point so the gap between them is as specified by the manufacturer.

NOTE

"Top dead center" refers to the position of the piston at the start of the ignition stroke, when the contact points open and spark is produced by the spark plug. But the piston has another top dead center—that's at the completion of the exhaust stroke when the breaker points are closed. To make sure the piston is at the correct top dead center, look at the breaker points. They should be open. If they are closed, turn the crankshaft through another revolution to bring the piston to the correct top dead center.

5. Place a clean index card between the open breaker points. Then, turn the crankshaft backwards until the points close and grip the paper.

6. Loosen the breaker point adjusting screw or bolt and carefully inch the points apart until the index card falls loose. Retighten the adjusting screw or bolt. Ignition timing is now set.

7. Reinstall the flywheel, spark plug, and spark plug cable.

COMPRESSION LOSS**

Compression is the force exerted by the piston on the fuel mixture during the compression stroke to reduce its volume. Without being compressed, the fuel mixture in the combustion chamber won't ignite and expel maximum energy to drive the piston and crankshaft.

A compression leak between two engine components because of wear or damage is responsible for a loss of compression. This loss can be detected with a compression gauge, which you can buy from an outdoor power equipment dealer. You also need the compression specification for your engine, which the dealer can provide. But before buying the gauge, tighten the cylinder head in case the compression loss is the result of a loose head.

To make a compression test, do the following:

1. Take the cable off the spark plug and remove the spark plug from the cylinder head.

2. Depending on the type of compression gauge you purchased, screw the nozzle of the gauge securely into the spark plug port or press the nozzle into the port as tightly as possible. If there is a loss of compression around the nozzle of the gauge because it isn't in the spark plug port securely enough, the reading you get on the gauge will show a reading that is lower than it really is, perhaps causing you to overhaul the engine unnecessarily.

3. Crank the engine or have an assistant crank the engine. If the engine has a manually operated rewind starter, keep pulling the rope until the needle of the compression gauge doesn't go any higher. If the engine is equipped with electric starting, keep the ignition switch engaged until the needle of the compression gauge doesn't go any higher.

4. Record the reading and compare it to the specification. A 10 percent difference from the specification is within normal limits. However, if the compression reading is low, do the test over again to make sure the reading you got is accurate before deciding that an engine overhaul is needed.

Repair

Overhaul the engine (see Chapter 12).

STARTING SYSTEM FAILURE

It is usually obvious when a faulty starting system component is keeping the engine from starting. Therefore, no troubleshooting procedure is necessary.

Engines of outdoor power machines have a rewind starter (also called a recoil starter), which is characterized by a rope that you pull, or an electric starting system that is similar to the one your car uses. Some engines have both, with the rewind starter serving as a backup if the electric starting system fails.

If the rope of a rewind starter snaps, you won't be able to start the engine until you replace the rope (see Chapter 11). If one of the parts of an electric starting system fails, there won't be any response from the engine when you engage the ignition key, or the engine will crank too sluggishly to start. As in your car, the components that make up an electric starting system are a battery, alternator, and starter motor (see Chapter 11).

DAMAGED FLYWHEEL KEY

A key (Figure 6.8) is in position between the flywheel and crankshaft for two purposes. One is to keep the flywheel in proper relation to the crankshaft. If the flywheel is not kept in a relative position to the crankshaft, ignition timing will be thrown off kilter and the engine may not start or will be hard to start.

The second job of the flywheel key is to protect the crankshaft if the working end of the outdoor power machine strikes an object with enough force to bend the crankshaft. Before this can happen, the flywheel key breaks away, releasing the hold that the flywheel has on the crankshaft. The crankshaft is prevented from receiving a damaging blow, because it is free of the restrictive force imposed on it by the flywheel.

Troubleshooting and Repair***

Remove the flywheel so you can examine the flywheel key, and replace the key if it is bent or broken in two. You need a flywheel puller, flywheel holder, and perhaps a clutch wrench

FIGURE 6.9. To remove the flywheel cover, release the rewind starter rope from the handlebar of the machine and cables that are attached to the cover.

and brake-band tang bending tool if the outdoor power machine is a self-propelled rotary lawn mower. These are comparatively inexpensive tools (about $20 for the four as this is being written) that you will probably use over and over again in caring for the engine. The tools are available from an outdoor power equipment dealer who sells your make of equipment. When you have them in hand, follow the steps illustrated in Figures 6.9 through 6.19, but keep in mind that there are variations between engines:

1. Disconnect the spark plug cable and point it away from the spark plug terminal.

2. Take out the air filter, take off the engine housing cover, and remove the flywheel cover (Figures 6.9 and 6.10).

3. Remove the screen over the flywheel. Be careful not to cut your hand on the sharp edges of the screen (Figure 6.11).

4. If there is a starter clutch over the flywheel, place a clutch wrench on it.

FIGURE 6.10.   Remove bolts to take off the cover.

FIGURE 6.11. To remove the flywheel screen from this machine, you have to remove the fly-wheel nut. To do that, hold the flywheel with the flywheel holder as you turn the nut.

Then, attach a lever bar to the clutch wrench. Place the flywheel holder in position to grasp the fins of the fly-wheel so the part won't move and loosen the starter clutch. After you remove the starter clutch, be sure to retrieve the washer under it.

5. If you haven't as yet taken off the fly-wheel nut, use an open-end or crescent wrench to loosen the nut and unscrew the nut until it covers the threads of the crankshaft. Don't remove the nut. Leave it in place over the threads. The purpose of keeping the flywheel nut in place is to protect the threads of the crankshaft as you remove the flywheel. If you hit the threads and damage them, you will have to replace the crankshaft.

6. Inspect the top of the flywheel for two holes. These are for the flywheel puller. If this is the first time that the flywheel is coming off the engine, these holes may not be threaded, but don't worry about that. The flywheel puller has self-tapping screws. As you turn the screws into the holes, they will thread the

holes. Attach the flywheel puller over the crankshaft so its screws are inserted in the two holes (Figure 6.12).

7. If this is a rotary self-propelled lawn mower, you probably have to release a flywheel brake. The brake stops the flywheel and, therefore, the blade from rotating when you take your hands off the handle of the mower. The reason for equipping lawn mower engines with this device is to prevent injuries, especially to children, that can result by leaving a mower unattended with the engine running.

Releasing the flywheel brake of the engine illustrated in Figures 6.13–6.15 is easy. Release the gripper that is on the handlebar. The brake will stay off the flywheel.

Releasing other types of flywheel brakes is a bit more complicated. Remove the cover that's over the brake. Then, using the tang bending tool, bend the tang on the side of the brake until it

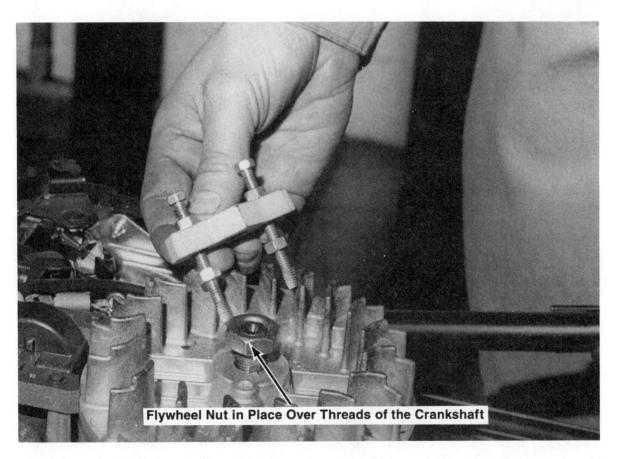

Flywheel Nut in Place Over Threads of the Crankshaft

FIGURE 6.12. Keeping the flywheel nut over the crankshaft to protect the threads, attach the flywheel puller to the flywheel.

FIGURE 6.13. The brake snaps against the flywheel when you take your hands off the handlebar and the engine is running.

no longer is in contact with the brake. Then, using a nut driver or needle-nose pliers, disconnect the spring. This releases the brake from the flywheel so you can proceed to remove the flywheel.

8. Tighten each bolt and nut on top of the puller alternately, a little at a time, until the bolts bottom out (Figure 6.16). Keep turning the bolts until you hear a pop, which means that the flywheel has come loose.

IMPORTANT

Do not strike the flywheel with a hammer to try and get it loose. If you shatter the magnets in the flywheel, which are necessary for producing voltage, break off one or more of the flywheel fins, or crack the flywheel, the part will have to be replaced.

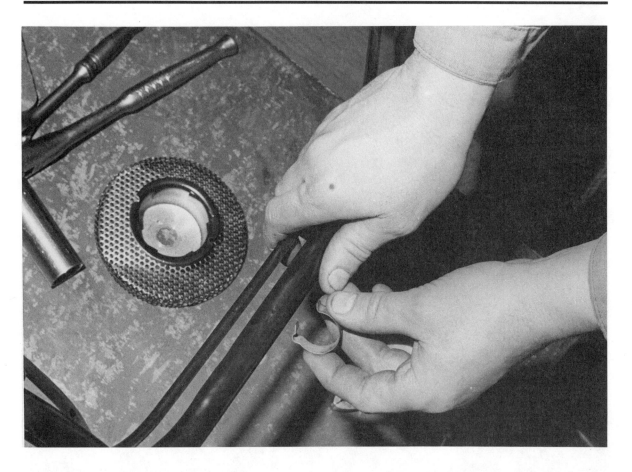

FIGURE 6.14.   Releasing the handlebar gripper of this machine will release the flywheel brake.

9. Remove the flywheel (Figure 6.17).

10. Retrieve and inspect the flywheel key (Figure 6.18). If it is bent or broken in two, get a new one. If there isn't any damage, the flywheel key is not the reason for the starting problem you are having.

11. To reattach the flywheel, install the flywheel key into the keyway in the crankshaft. Then, line up the flywheel so the key falls into the keyway and press the key down (Figure 6.19).

12. Reassemble the parts you removed. When it comes to the flywheel nut, screw the nut on and tighten it with a torque wrench to manufacturer specification, which can be anywhere from 35 to 145 ft.-lbs. The dealer who sells you the flywheel removal tools can tell you the specification.

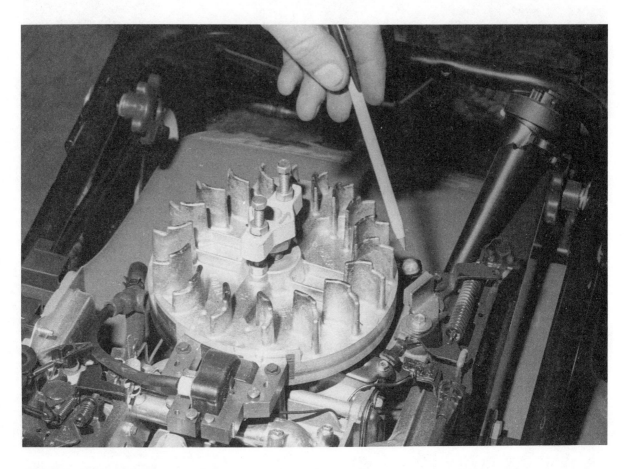

FIGURE 6.15. The brake will stay away from the flywheel, which allows you to take the fly-wheel off the engine.

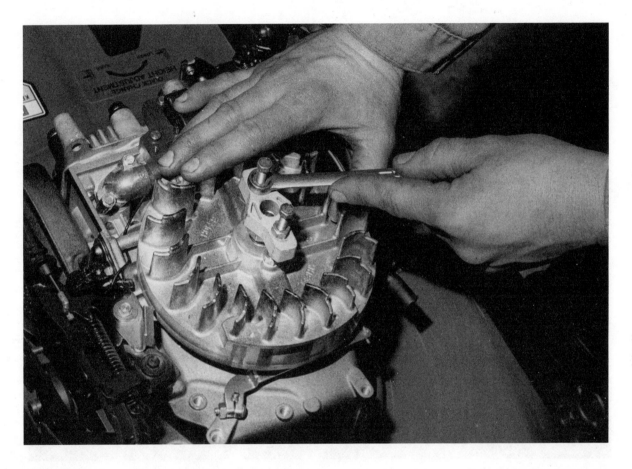

FIGURE 6.16. Tighten the bolts of the flywheel puller alternately to get the flywheel off the crankshaft.

Flywheel Key

FIGURE 6.17.   Remove the flywheel. Notice the flywheel key in the crankshaft.

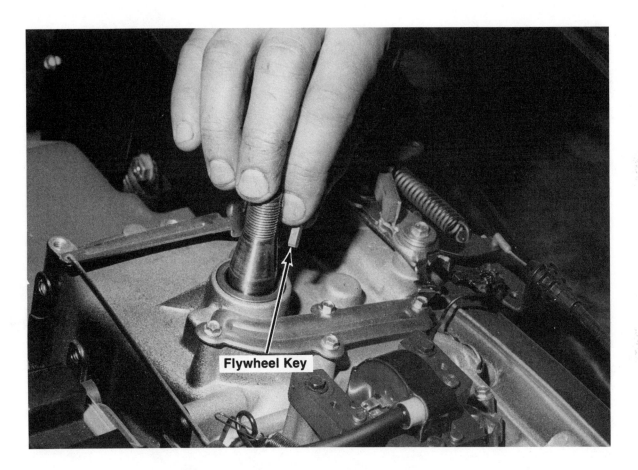

Flywheel Key

FIGURE 6.18.   Remove and inspect the flywheel key.

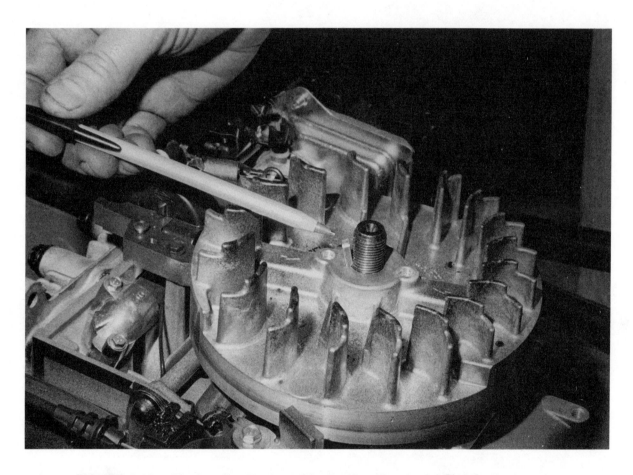

FIGURE 6.19.   The key fits in slots (keyways) in the crankshaft and flywheel.

7

Troubleshooting and Repairing a Flaw in Engine Performance

In the context used here, the term "engine performance flaw" covers one of the following conditions:

- The engine loses power. There is a drop in power that you can feel or hear when you put the outdoor power machine under a load, such as mowing a lawn, tilling soil, or removing snow. If the power loss is sharp enough, the engine will stall.

- The engine misses. An engine that misses (runs unevenly) is one that skips when it is idling or when the equipment is put under a load. The engine may stall.

- The engine stalls. The engine runs without displaying a power loss or miss, but stalls without warning.

- The engine surges. The speed of the engine alternately increases and decreases, as if the engine can't make up its mind at which speed to run.

These engine performance flaws are discussed as a group in this chapter because most of the causes are common to more than one of the flaws. The chart that follows spells out which flaws are most likely to result from which malfunction.

As in previous chapters, tasks described in this chapter are rated with one *, two **, or three ***. One * designates a job that a novice do-it-yourselfer can probably do. Two ** indicate a job that requires some do-it-yourself experience. Three *** suggest tasks for which advanced do-it-yourself experience is needed.

Guide to Troubleshooting Engine Performance Flaws

Malfunction	Performance Flaw	What to Do	Refer to
Out of gas	Stalling	Fill the fuel tank	—
Obstructed fuel cap vent	Power loss, missing, surging	Open the fuel cap vent	Chapter 3, page 45
Dirty air filter	Power loss, missing, surging	Service the air filter	Chapter 3, pages 45–52
Low oil level	Power loss, missing, stalling	Fill the crankcase	—
Gasoline is contaminated	Power loss, missing, stalling	Drain contaminated gasoline	Chapter 6, pages 81–84
Fouled or damaged spark plug	Power loss, missing, stalling	Service the spark plug	Chapter 3, pages 36–39
Clogged muffler	Power loss, missing, stalling	Service the muffler	This chapter, page 103
Fuel line is partially clogged	Stalling	Clean out an obstructed fuel line	This chapter, page 105
Idling speed is off the mark	Stalling	Adjust idling speed	Chapter 3, pages 52–53
Carburetor is clogged	Power loss, missing, stalling	Clean the carburetor	This chapter, page 105
Ignition breakdown	Power loss, missing, stalling	Test the ignition system	Chapter 3, page 36
Damaged Spark plug cable	Power loss, missing, stalling	Troubleshoot the spark plug cable	Chapter 6, pages 85–86

Guide to Troubleshooting Engine Performance Flaws

Malfunction	Performance Flaw	What to Do	Refer to
Ignition timing is off the mark	Power loss, missing, stalling	Adjust ignition timing	Chapter 6, pages 86–88
Compression loss	Power loss, missing, stalling	Test compression	Chapter 6, pages 88–89
Carbon in the engine	Power loss, missing, stalling	Do a power tune-up	Chapter 4, pages 63–68
Fuel screen is clogged	Surging	Clean the fuel screen	This chapter, pages 105–106
Sticking governor	Power loss, missing, stalling	Service the governor	This chapter, pages 106–108
Valve adjustment is off the mark	Power loss	Adjust the valves	This chapter, pages 108–110
Flywheel key is damaged	Power loss, missing, stalling	Replace the flywheel key	Chapter 6, pages 90–95
Crankshaft is bent	Power loss, missing, stalling	Overhaul the engine	This chapter, page 110, Chapter 12, pages 149–152

CLOGGED MUFFLER

A one-cylinder four-stroke engine is outfitted with a muffler that is held to the engine by bolts or is threaded into the engine (Figure 7.1). The muffler reduces the noise that an engine makes. If a muffler gets clogged with dirt or carbon, or if it is dented, back pressure alters engine performance and the engine will run poorly.

Troubleshooting and Repair**

1. Make sure the engine is cold and unbolt or unscrew the muffler. If you touch a hot muffler, you will get a severe burn.

2. Start the engine. If the engine now runs flawlessly, the problem you have been experiencing is being caused by the muffler.

3. Inspect the muffler. If it is crushed, buy a new muffler from a dealer who sells your make of outdoor power equipment. Bolt or screw the new part to the engine.

4. Assuming that the muffler is not crushed, use a long screwdriver to scrape out dirt and carbon. Tapping the muffler with a rubber or plastic mallet will also loosen debris.

5. Bolt or screw the part to the engine and start the engine. If servicing the old muffler hasn't resulted in a better running engine, replace the muffler.

Muffler

FIGURE 7.1.   All engines have mufflers. A damaged muffler can cause an engine performance problem.

OBSTRUCTED FUEL LINE

Where there is a fuel line between the fuel tank and carburetor, the possibility exists that a clogged fuel line, or one that is pinched or kinked, is restricting the flow of gasoline to the engine.

Troubleshooting and Repair**

Examine the fuel line to make sure it isn't pinched or kinked. If you can't straighten the line, replace it. To clean the fuel line, do this:

1. Remove the spark plug cable from the spark plug and point the end of the cable away from the plug.
2. Hold a can under the fuel line as you disconnect it from the carburetor. If gasoline doesn't flow freely from the end of the line, pinch off the end of the line, use a syringe to drain the fuel tank (see Chapter 6), and continue with this procedure. A free flow of gasoline means that the line is clear so look elsewhere for the cause of the performance problem.
3. Disconnect the fuel line from the fuel tank.
4. Clean out the line by pushing a soft patch through it. Be careful not to poke a hole in the line.
5. Reconnect the line to the fuel tank and carburetor.

CLOGGED CARBURETOR

Judging whether a carburetor is partially clogged so it isn't delivering enough gasoline to the engine is difficult. When this condition arises, the engine will start, but it will lack power, miss, and/or stall.

Since it is difficult to establish the existence of a lean-running condition—that is, an insufficient quantity of gasoline in the fuel mixture brought about by a clogged carburetor—assume that the problem you are having is being caused by a clogged carburetor and make the simple repair described below. If this doesn't work, tackle the other reasons listed in the chart for lack of power, missing, and/or stalling before concluding that internal parts of the carburetor, such as the jets, are so badly clogged that they resist cleaning, and that the only way to alleviate the problem is to overhaul the carburetor (see Chapter 10).

Repair**

Proceed as follows:

1. Uncover the carburetor throat.
2. Following directions on the container, pour carburetor cleaner down the throat of the carburetor.
3. Start the engine and let it run at idle for the period of time called for by the directions.

Carburetor cleaners are available from outdoor power equipment dealers and also from dealers of automobile parts and supplies. If one treatment with the cleaner doesn't work, try another before giving it up as a lost cause.

THE FUEL SCREEN

Fuel systems are equipped with fuel screens to filter out dirt that may be introduced into the carburetor with gasoline. Dirt can clog a carburetor.

If your machine has a fuel line between the fuel tank and carburetor, there probably is a conically shaped screen in the bottom of the tank to trap dirt. If the carburetor sits on top of the fuel tank, the bottoms of the pickup pipes that extend into the fuel tank from the carburetor are equipped with screens.

Troubleshooting and Repair**

For a screen that is positioned in the bottom of the fuel tank, proceed as follows:

1. Disconnect the spark plug cable and point it away from the spark plug terminal.
2. Drain the fuel tank and take it off the engine.
3. Remove the screen by unscrewing its fitting from the bottom of the tank.
4. Wash the screen in carburetor cleaner or a suitable product recommended by a dealer of outdoor power equipment. Then, let it dry.
5. Place the screen back into the tank, using a new gasket, and tighten the fitting.
6. Install the tank back on the engine and fill it with gasoline.
7. Make sure there isn't any leak from around the fitting. If there is a leak, tighten the fitting a little more. If you can't get the leak to stop, the gasket has probably been damaged. Drain the tank again, remove the screen, install another gasket, and secure the screen to the tank.

If your machine has the carburetor sitting on top of the fuel tank, proceed as follows:

1. Disconnect the spark plug cable and point it away from the spark plug terminal.
2. Unscrew the carburetor from the fuel tank and lift it off (Figure 7.2).
3. Clean the screens in the bottoms of the fuel pickup pipes by soaking them in carburetor cleaner or an agent recommended by a dealer of outboard power equipment to dissolve dirt (Figure 7.3).

NOTE

If the screens are so badly clogged that they don't come clean, replace the fuel pipes (see Chapter 10).

---

4. Reinstall the carburetor.

CAUTION

Since you're working in the presence of gasoline, remember not to smoke or bring anything that can cause a spark near the machine.

THE GOVERNOR

The job of the governor is to help the engine maintain a constant speed despite variations in the load imposed on the engine by the outdoor power machine. The governor also keeps the engine from overspeeding when the load is relieved.

There are several variations of governors. One of the most popular is a mechanical unit

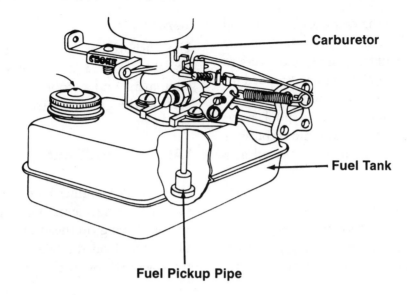

FIGURE 7.2. If the carburetor on an outdoor power machine is on top of the fuel tank, fuel is delivered to the carburetor through fuel pickup pipes. There is a screen at the base of each pickup pipe to block the entry of dirt into the carburetor.

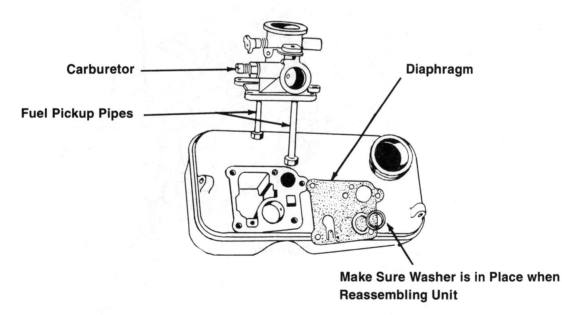

FIGURE 7.3. Remove the carburetor from the fuel tank and clean the screen in the base of each pickup pipe. Note the diaphragm illustrated here. It acts as a fuel pump to deliver fuel from the tank into the carburetor through the pickup pipes. Replace this diaphragm if it is damaged.

that is attached to the crankshaft at one end and to the carburetor throttle valve at the other. It uses weights, springs, and levers to control the speed of the engine. As speed increases, centrifugal force moves the weights outward. This action releases a spool, moving a series of levers that close the carburetor throttle accordingly to maintain speed at a governed pace.

There isn't any troubleshooting procedure that will tell you if the governor is malfunctioning. When a performance flaw occurs that might be caused by a dirty governor, you have to assume the governor is at fault.

Repair*

Use carburetor cleaner or a similar agent available from a dealer of outdoor power equipment and a toothbrush to clean the parts of the governor assembly.

VALVE ADJUSTMENT

One-cylinder engines have one of two kinds of valve arrangements. One type is used in engines having overhead valves (Figure 7.4). The spring-loaded intake and exhaust valves are operated by rocker arms. The rocker

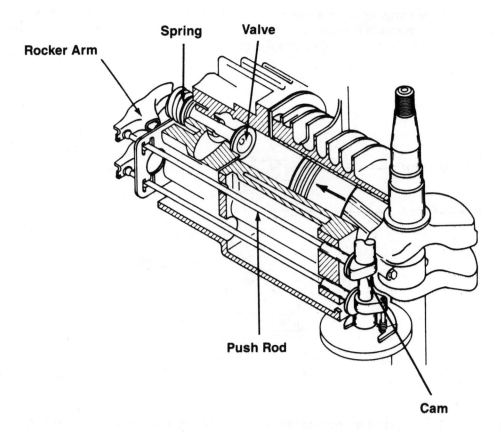

FIGURE 7.4. This cutaway drawing of a one-cylinder overhead valve engine shows the parts of the valve train. The intake and exhaust valves can be adjusted to compensate for wear.

arms are operated by push rods that are activated by the camshaft. This kind of arrangement can be adjusted to compensate for valve wear.

The other kind of valve arrangement, sometimes referred to as a poppet valve train, cannot be adjusted. The components that make up the valve train run in a straight line from the cylinder head to the camshaft. About three-quarters of the way between the head and camshaft, the stems of the valves meet tappets. Also at this point are springs that allow the valves to open and close as the tappets put pressure on the valve stems and then release pressure. This pressure is applied and relieved by the cams of the camshaft on which the tappets ride. Although poppet valves cannot be adjusted, they can be checked for wear.

As valves begin to wear, the clearance between them and the cylinder head becomes greater. This can lead to a loss of compression, which reduces the power output of the engine. Worn valves cause an engine to knock.

*Troubleshooting***

To determine whether the clearance between the valves and the cylinder head exceeds specification, indicating excessive wear, do the following:

1. Disconnect the cable from the spark plug and remove the spark plug.
2. Insert a wood dowel in the spark plug port so it comes into contact with the top of the piston and rotate the crankshaft to bring the piston to top dead center (see Chapter 6). The valves must be closed when you measure clearance.

IMPORTANT
The engine must be cold.

3. Remove the bolts from the valve cover and discard the old gasket. You will need a new gasket, so buy one before you start the job. At that time, ask the dealer who sells the make of engine for the valve clearance specifications for your particular engine. The clearance for the intake valve, which is the larger of the two, and the clearance for the exhaust valve are often different so be sure to get both specs.
4. If you have an overhead valve engine, slip a feeler gauge that corresponds to the specified valve clearance between the top of the valve stem and the underside of the

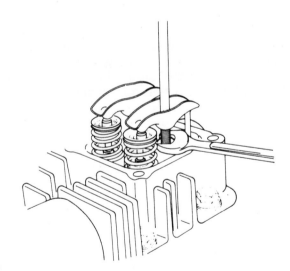

FIGURE 7.5. To adjust valves of a one-cylinder overhead valve engine, hold the rocker arm screw with a screwdriver as you loosen the rocker arm nut.

rocker arm. Slide the feeler gauge back and forth. If it moves without offering ample resistance, the valve is worn, but you might be able to adjust it to compensate for wear. To do that, loosen the rocker arm and move it the required distance to get the correct setting between it and the valve stem (Figure 7.5). Then, tighten the rocker arm to specification

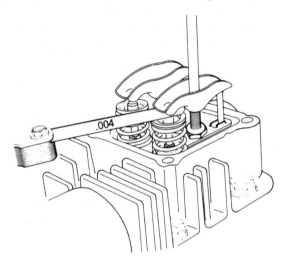

FIGURE 7.6. Adjust the valves by turning the rocker arm screw until the gap between the rocker arm and the top of the push rod is in line with the manufacturer's specification.

(Figure 7.6). Again, you will have to get this spec from a dealer who sells your make of equipment.

5. If your engine has a poppet valve arrangement, slip the correct size feeler gauge between the valve stem and tappet. Move the gauge back and forth. You should feel ample resistance. If not, the valve is worn and should be replaced (see Chapter 12).

A BENT CRANKSHAFT

If for some reason a flywheel key doesn't give way when an outdoor power machine strikes an object (see Chapter 6), the crankshaft can bend. This is the most serious damage that an engine can incur. When it happens, a machine is usually discarded, because the cost of having a new crankshaft installed by a professional technician almost equals the cost of new equipment. A new crankshaft is not particularly expensive, but the time required to do the job is costly if a technician is hired. However, if you can do the work yourself, the cost is reduced (see Chapter 12).

8

Troubleshooting and Repairing
Other Engine Problems

This chapter outlines troubleshooting procedures to follow when you are trying to correct a number of engine problems including overheating, excessive vibration, knocking, or motor oil consumption. Remember as you go through this chapter that one * indicates a task that novice do-it-yourselfers should be able to handle, two ** are tasks that do-it-yourselfers with some experience can do, and three *** are jobs requiring advanced do-it-yourself experience.

AN ENGINE THAT OVERHEATS

Unlike cars, outdoor power machines are not equipped with gauges or lights that warn operators that engine temperature is approaching dangerous levels. But like a car engine that overheats, major damage to the engine of an outdoor power machine can result if overheating isn't recognized and steps taken to eliminate the problem.

Since outdoor power machines don't have warning devices, owners should be on the lookout for two symptoms suggesting that overheating may be occurring: (1) The engine, when warmed up, stalls; (2) the engine, when warmed up, is hard to restart after it has been turned off for a few minutes. When one of these conditions arises, and with the engine still warm, bring your hand slowly toward the cylinder head to see if heat is radiating from that part. Be careful not to touch it. You could get a severe burn. If you feel intense heat, the engine is overheating.

Guide to Troubleshooting an Engine That Overheats

Possible Cause	What to Do	Refer to
Excessive load being put on the engine	Check the owner's manual for correct usage	—
Dirt-clogged cylinder head	Clean the cylinder head	Chapter 2, page 30
Low crankcase oil level	Fill the crankcase	—
Oil is contaminated	Change the oil	Chapter 2, pages 28–30
Dirty air filter	Service the air filter	Chapter 3, pages 45–52
Clogged muffler	Service the muffler	Chapter 7, page 103
Carbon in the engine	Do a power tune-up	Chapter 4, pages 63–68

EXCESSIVE VIBRATION

The following engine-related problems can result in excessive vibration:

- A broken flywheel. Inspect and replace the flywheel, if necessary (see Chapter 6).
- A bent crankshaft. Disassemble the engine, examine the crankshaft, and install a new crankshaft, if necessary (see Chapter 12).

When excessive vibration occurs, the engine may not be malfunctioning. In fact, more often than not, vibration results when an engine isn't mounted securely to the deck of the equipment or an attachment, particularly a lawn mower blade, is damaged and unbalanced. Therefore, first tighten every bolt you can find. Then, start the engine to see if the vibration has been eliminated or reduced. If there isn't any difference and the machine is a lawn mower, check and repair the blade as follows:

Troubleshooting and Repairing a Lawn Mower Blade**

Replace a blade that is bent or badly gouged. It cannot be restored.

If the blade is worn or nicked, it can be sharpened and kept in use. Here's how to do this job:

1. Release the spark plug cable and point it away from the spark plug.

2. Drain the fuel tank of gasoline and the crankcase of oil.

3. Turn the mower on its end to get at the blade, but first check the owner's manual to determine on what end the manufacturer wants you to turn it. Generally, Briggs and Stratton engines should be positioned with the spark plug facing up. Tecumseh engines should be positioned with the spark plug facing down. This is to prevent residual fuel from running into the air filter housing.

4. Remove the center bolt, take the blade off the crankshaft, and mount the blade in a bench vise. Make sure you retrieve the washer(s) and hub, if they are used, as well as the bolt.

5. Holding a single bastard file at an angle that coincides with the bevel of the blade, stroke across one of the cutting edges until nicks in the blade are smooth. As you do, count the number of strokes. Then, repeat the filing on the other cutting edge for that number of strokes. This is done to maintain balance. This is the reason for counting the strokes and applying the same number to cutting edges. It is a very important step and should not be discounted.

6. After doing step 5, take the blade out of the vise and stick a pencil through the center hole or place the blade on a blade balancing mechanism. You can buy this

tool, which resembles a pyramid, from a power mower dealer. Let the blade come to rest.

7. If the blade doesn't lie evenly, but leans toward the heavy side, mount it in the vise again and give that side one or two stokes with the file. Then, test balance again. Repeat the procedure until balance is attained.

8. Mount the blade in the vise and sharpen it with a drill-mounted honing stone. Make three or four passes along one edge; then, the same number of passes along the other edge.

9. Check the balance again.

10. After the blade has been balanced, put it back on the mower, reinstall the washer(s) and hub, screw on the center bolt, and tighten it.

ENGINE KNOCK

An engine knock may indicate nothing more serious than the need to do a power tune-up or adjust intake and exhaust valves. On the other hand, a knock may mean that major damage exists inside the engine. (See guide at the top of page 114.)

FIND THE CAUSE OF EXCESSIVE OIL CONSUMPTION

An engine should not need replenishment of its oil supply between oil changes. If you have to add oil frequently, you need to determine whether the problem is easily solved or if the excessive oil consumption is a sign of

Guide to Troubleshooting an Engine That Knocks

Possible Cause	What to Do	Refer to
Carbon in the engine	Do a power tune-up	Chapter 4, pages 63–68
Loose flywheel	Tighten the flywheel nut to specification	Chapter 6, page 95
Valve adjustment is off the mark	Adjust the valves	Chapter 7, pages 108–110
Internal damage to engine	Overhaul the engine	Chapter 12, pages 149–152

major engine damage. (See the guide at the bottom of page.)

Reduce Oil Overfill*

Make sure the oil dipstick is fully seated and check the oil level. If it is above the FULL mark, the crankcase is too full. The excess oil is overflowing and being expelled through the breather system. Drain off the excess by changing the oil (see Chapter 2). Make sure the engine is filled with the correct amount of oil by using the dipstick to verify that the oil level is on or slightly below the FULL mark.

Repair the Crankcase Breather**

The crankcase breather maintains a partial vacuum in the crankcase, which is needed to keep oil from being forced past the piston rings into the combustion chamber where it will be burned with the fuel mixture. Crankcase breathers have filters. If the filter is clogged, the vacuum can be disrupted and a loss of oil will result.

There are various types of crankcase breathers, including a top-mounted breather at the rear of the engine block and a side-mounted breather over the valve compartment. The air filter housings of some engines also act as crankcase breathers. Consult your

Guide to Troubleshooting an Engine That Uses Too Much Oil

Possible Cause	What to Do	Refer to
Too much oil in engine	Reduce oil overfill	This chapter, page 114
Crankcase drain plug is loose	Tighten the plug	—
Oil filler cap gasket is damaged allowing oil to leak around the cap	Replace the oil filler cap	—
Clogged crankcase breather	Repair the crankcase breather	This chapter, pages 114–115
Internal damage to engine	Overhaul the engine	Chapter 12, pages 149–152

owner's manual or check with a dealer who sells your make of engine to determine the arrangement of the crankcase breather.

Usually the breather does not require servicing unless there are signs that the engine is starting to use oil. At that point, remove the hose from the breather housing cover and take off the cover. As you proceed, make a sketch of how the crankcase breather is assembled so you will be able to reassemble it correctly. If parts are installed incorrectly, the breather will fail to do its job and oil loss will be significant.

Discard the breather housing cover gasket and get a new one. Take out the filter. If it is the type that can be cleaned and reused, wash it in carburetor solvent. If it isn't reusable, get a new one. Reassemble the breather.

9

Working on the Ignition System

Engines of outdoor power machines have either a solid-state (also called electronic and capacitor discharge) or magneto (also called breaker point and contact point) ignition system (Figure 9.1). A solid-state ignition system doesn't have any moving parts. A magneto ignition system has breaker points that constantly fluctuate to open and close so the ignition system can produce the voltage needed by the spark plug to ignite the fuel mixture in the engine combustion chamber.

Solid-state ignition is maintenance-free and seldom fails. The module that helps to produce voltage for the spark plug is sealed so it can't be damaged by dirt, water, and oil—elements that can attack the breaker points of a magneto ignition system and

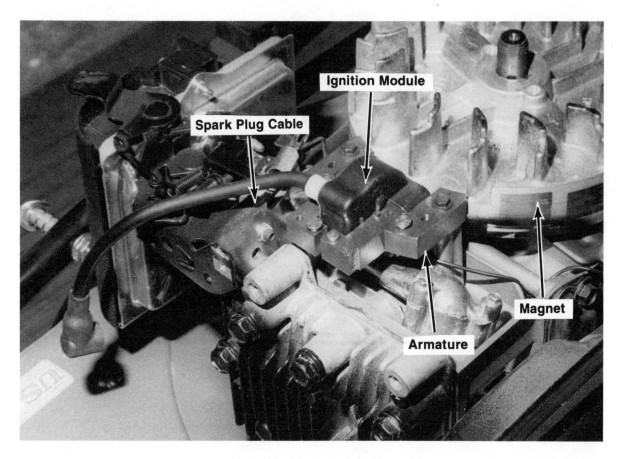

FIGURE 9.1. The solid-state ignition system of a one-cylinder engine features an encapsulated ignition module (coil) in an armature. Every time the flywheel magnets sweep past the armature, the module delivers current to the spark plug.

cause them to fail prematurely. Even if dirt, water, and oil never reach the breaker points, they still wear and require adjustment and eventual replacement, because over the course of their useful existence breaker points open and close millions of times.

The condenser is another part of a magneto ignition system that requires attention. The condenser absorbs random electricity and protects the breaker points from arcing. Arcing refers to flashes of current that resemble lightning. If it weren't for the fact

that arcs of current are absorbed by the condenser, they would streak across the breaker points as the points open, causing the points to burn and erode. You would then have to replace the points much more often than the period recommended by the manufacturer, which is every 150 hours that the engine is operated. A condenser should be replaced when the points are replaced. This will ensure adequate protection for the new breaker points.

CONVERTING A MAGNETO IGNITION SYSTEM

Practically all engines manufactured since 1983 have solid-state ignition systems. Those engines manufactured prior to this and some manufactured afterward have magneto ignition systems.

If your outdoor power machine is equipped with a Briggs and Stratton engine that has a magneto ignition system, you can probably convert that system to the Briggs and Stratton solid-state ignition system, which is called Magnetron, thus eliminating the drawbacks presented by magneto ignition. The project will take you about one hour to do. The price for the Magnetron parts kit, which can be obtained from a dealer who sells outdoor power machines equipped with Briggs and Stratton engines, is reasonable (about $20 as this was written).

The Magnetron parts kit contains a solid-state module, an aluminum flywheel key, and a stop-switch wire. You need the stop-switch wire if your machine is equipped with a stop-switch, which turns the engine off automatically when you release pressure on the handle-bar.

The solid-state module in conjunction with magnets of the rotating engine flywheel function as a switch to open and close the ignition coil primary circuit in the same way that the breaker points of a magneto ignition system do. The ignition coil is the same ignition coil that is presently in place in the magneto ignition system of your Briggs and Stratton engine. It converts low voltage (primary) current to high voltage (secondary) current that jumps the electrode gap of the spark plug to make the spark needed for igniting the fuel mixture. This current is transmitted to the spark plug through the spark plug cable, which is an integral part of the ignition coil.

The first step that should be taken to switch from a Briggs and Stratton magneto ignition system to a Magnetron solid-state ignition system is to determine whether the engine is eligible for conversion. It probably is since only 1 percent of the Briggs and Stratton engines manufactured since 1963, specifically cast-iron engines, cannot be converted. If you want to verify the status of your engine, jot down the model of the engine and ask a dealer who sells equipment having Briggs and Stratton engines.

Switching to Magnetron**

NOTE
The two ** given this project mean that the task is for a do-it-yourselfer who has some experience.

To install the Magnetron solid-state ignition system on your Briggs and Stratton engine, proceed as follows:

1. Disconnect the spark plug cable and point it away from the spark plug terminal.
2. Drain the fuel tank if you have to remove the tank to take off the flywheel.
3. Remove the flywheel (see Chapter 6).
4. Notice that the ignition coil has two parts—the coil itself and an armature that surrounds it. The coil sits inside the two legs of the armature. Notice also

that there are three or four wires attached to the coil. These are an ignition primary wire that extends from the coil to the breaker points, which are probably concealed by a dust cover; a wire that has an eyelet at one end that is bolted to the engine—this is the ground wire; the spark plug cable; possibly a stop-switch wire that extends from the coil to the terminal of the stop switch.

5. Use wire cutters to cut the ignition primary wire as close as possible to the breaker point dust cover. Also cut the stop-switch wire as close as possible to the ignition coil.

6. Take off the two bolts that hold the ignition coil and armature to the engine. Save the bolts. You will need them to attach the ignition coil, armature, and Magnetron module to the engine once you have combined these parts into one assembly.

7. Measure the ignition primary wire back three inches from the ignition coil and cut the wire at this point. Strip off $5/8$ inch of insulation from the end of the wire that is still attached to the ignition coil. Then, carefully scrape off the varnish from this end of the wire.

8. Press the Magnetron module onto the angular part of one of the legs of the armature, making certain that the module locks itself to the leg.

9. Notice that there is a spring-loaded terminal in the barrel part of the Magnetron module to which the ignition primary wire, new stop-switch wire (if the equipment has a stop-switch), and the wire connected to the Magnetron

module have to be connected. The Magnetron has two wires attached to it. The one that doesn't have the eyelet is the one that is to be combined with the others and attached to the spring-loaded terminal. The other wire—the one with the eyelet—is a ground wire.

10. Hold the tip of a ballpoint pen against the spring-loaded terminal and press the terminal to hold it open as you slide the ends of the wires under the terminal. When you have done this, remove the ballpoint pen so the terminal closes and locks the wires in place. Now, twist the wires together and solder them with $60/40$ rosin core solder. Don't let the hot soldering iron touch the plastic body of the Magnetron module. It will melt.

11. Twist together the ground wire attached to the ignition coil and the ground wire attached to the Magnetron module and solder these two using $60/40$ rosin core solder. Cut off one of the two ground wires as close to the soldered connection as possible, because only one ground wire is needed.

12. To keep wires from vibrating and possibly breaking as you operate the outdoor power machine, cement them to the body of the ignition coil by spreading Permatex on the coil and sticking the wires into the Permatex. Use plenty of Permatex, which can be purchased in a hardware store. It won't harm the coil or the wires.

13. Position the ignition coil-armature-Magnetron module assembly on the engine, and bring the ground wire over the top of the assembly so the eyelet is accessible. Using the two bolts you

saved, mount the assembly to the engine, slipping one of the bolts through the eyelet of the ground wire. Tighten both bolts.

NOTE

If your engine has a metal air vane, you may have to cut or grind the air vane bracket a bit to obtain clearance so the assembly will fit into the space.

---

14. Disconnect the old stop-switch wire from the stop-switch terminal. Extend the new stop-switch wire over the same route that the original wire took and connect it to the stop-switch terminal.

15. Discard the old flywheel key and replace it with the new key from the Magnetron parts kit. The old key is probably made of zinc. The new key is a more durable aluminum.

16. Install the flywheel. Using a torque wrench, tighten the flywheel nut to the specification required by your engine. You can get this spec from a dealer who sells outdoor power equipment outfitted with Briggs and Stratton engines.

17. Set the armature-to-flywheel air gap to the specification for your engine (ask the dealer). This gap is the ideal spacing between the armature and flywheel that is needed by the ignition coil to build up secondary voltage. To do this, loosen the bolts so you can move the coil-armature-Magnetron module assembly (Figure 9.2). Hold a feeler gauge corresponding to the air gap spec between one leg of the armature and the flywheel. Move the assembly until it comes against the feeler gauge. Then, tighten the bolts.

18. Reinstall the other parts you had to take off to do the conversion. Then, start the engine. If it won't start, you made a mistake doing the installation. Recheck your work.

NOTE

You may have noticed that no mention has been made of what to do about the old breaker points and condenser. You can leave them just where they are.

HOW MAGNETO IGNITION WORKS

A magneto ignition system is composed of magnets that are part of the flywheel, a coil and armature assembly, breaker points, and a condenser. The coil is a transformer that is capable of converting low voltage to the high voltage that is needed to jump the gap between the spark plug electrodes. This produces an intense spark.

The ignition coil consists of thousands of turns (coils) of fine and heavy wire referred to as the primary and secondary windings, respectively. They are wrapped around a metal core. One end of the secondary winding is connected to the spark plug. This is the spark plug cable.

As the flywheel rotates, the magnets sweep past the coil and armature assembly, creating

FIGURE 9.2. Adjust the air gap between the flywheel and armature leg at either of the spots shown in this photograph. The gap is set by loosening the bolts and moving the armature.

a magnetic field that produces a flow of low voltage (200 to 300 volts) through the primary winding of the coil. One end of the primary winding is connected by a wire to the movable point of the breaker point assembly.

As the magnets in the flywheel sweep past the coil and armature assembly, the breaker points are closed. The movable point is controlled by the rotation of the crankshaft. As the crankshaft turns to bring the raised part of a cam under the movable point, the point opens. This cuts off the flow of low voltage

to the primary winding. Simultaneously, the low voltage flowing through the primary winding is induced into the secondary winding as the magnetic field collapses. The high voltage (about 10,000 volts) which is created in the secondary winding as a result of this action is routed through the spark plug cable to the spark plug.

Any part of a magneto ignition system can go bad. The parts that cause most of the problems, though, are the spark plug cable and the breaker points.

NOTE

One * indicates a project that a novice do-it-yourselfer can probably do. Two ** indicate a project for a do-it-yourselfer who has some experience.

Repair a Damaged Spark Plug Cable* or **

You might be able to salvage a cracked spark plug cable and, therefore, the ignition coil by wrapping the cable with electrician's tape. This is a one * task. If this doesn't work, you will have to replace the ignition coil, by removing the flywheel. This task is rated two **.

NOTE

This repair is also necessary for a damaged spark plug cable of a solid-state ignition system.

Replace Worn Breaker Points and the Condenser**

1. Disconnect the spark plug cable and point it away from the spark plug.
2. Drain the fuel tank if that is necessary to remove the flywheel.
3. Remove the flywheel (see Chapter 6).
4. If a dust cover is used to protect the breaker points, take it off.
5. Determine how the breaker points and condenser are attached. Remove them.
6. Install new points and condenser.
7. Using a feeler gauge of the correct size, adjust the spacing between the points to the specification laid down by the manufacturer, which is probably 0.020 inch (see Chapter 6).
8. Reinstall the dust cover and the flywheel. Make sure the flywheel key is in its proper position.
9. Tighten the flywheel nut to the manufacturer's specification. You can find out what this is by checking with a dealer who sells your make of equipment.
10. Reinstall the other parts you removed.

10

Working on the
Carburetor

The engine of an outdoor power machine has either a gravity- or suction-feed carburetor.

A gravity-feed carburetor has the fuel tank above the carburetor so gasoline flows into the carburetor bowl. A float system keeps the bowl from overflowing.

A suction-feed carburetor has the carburetor above the fuel tank. Air rushing through the carburetor air horn creates a partial vacuum in the carburetor that pulls gasoline up from the fuel tank through one or two pipes immersed in gasoline that are attached to the carburetor. Some suction-feed carburetors on higher horsepower engines are equipped with a diaphragm. This flexible device is exposed to engine intake manifold pressure on one side and to atmospheric pressure on the other side, resulting in a pulsation that assists in drawing the quantity of fuel from the tank into the carburetor that is needed by bigger engines to operate under the higher loads usually imposed on these engines.

LOOKING FOR ENGINE TROUBLE

The cause of an engine problem usually lies outside rather than inside the carburetor. If all the techniques discussed in previous chapters has failed to resolve the trouble you are having with an engine, and you are dealing with a gravity-feed carburetor, determine if the float system is causing the difficulty before overhauling the entire carburetor. This is a two ** task—that is, a do-it-yourselfer with some experience should be able to do it.

After the float system has been tested and repaired, or if the carburetor is a suction-feed unit, the only other procedure that remains is to remove the carburetor from the engine and take it apart for cleaning and overhaul. This task gets three ***, because it requires advanced do-it-yourself experience.

REPAIR THE CARBURETOR FLOAT SYSTEM**

The carburetor float system consists of a float and a needle valve (Figure 10.1). Together, they control the amount of gasoline that enters the carburetor bowl from the fuel tank.

The system works similarly to a home toilet tank. When the quantity of gasoline in the carburetor bowl is below normal level, the float drops and pulls the needle valve off an entry point called the seat. This allows gasoline to enter the bowl from the fuel tank. As the level of gasoline rises in the bowl, it raises the float and drops the needle valve back into the seat, which shuts off the flow of gasoline into the bowl. The things that can go wrong with this system are:

- The hollow float develops a leak and gasoline gets into it. This makes for a heavy float. The abnormally weighty part can't rise to normal level. The needle valve, therefore, won't seal the entry point. Gasoline rises in the bowl and may overflow if the condition is bad enough. In addition, excess gasoline can enter the cylinder, flooding it and causing hard engine starting.

- Dirt gets on the needle valve or into the seat so the entry point is never closed off. This causes gasoline to continually drip into the bowl, resulting in an over-rich fuel condition. A worn needle valve causes the same problem.

The following steps can serve as a guide in helping to check on and repair the float system of a gravity-feed carburetor:

CAUTION

Remember, you will be working in the presence of gasoline so take the necessary safety precautions. Do not smoke or bring anything near the area that may create a spark.

---

1. Disconnect the spark plug cable and point it away from the spark plug terminal.

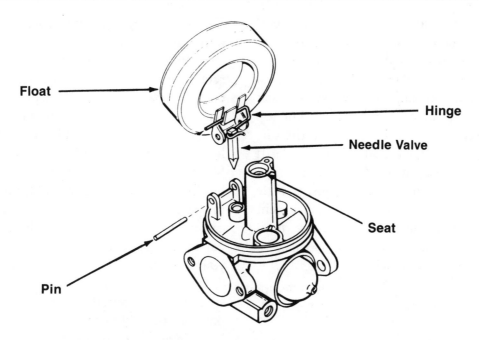

Float — **Hinge**

Needle Valve

Seat

Pin

**FIGURE 10.1.   A float and needle valve of a gravity feed carburetor controls the flow of gaso-
line. The float and needle valve are hinged and kept attached to the carburetor bowl by the
hinge pin.**

2. Close off the fuel flow to the carburetor and remove the carburetor from the
engine.

3. Drain the carburetor bowl by removing
the drain plug, pressing the drain screw,
or opening the petcock.

4. Unscrew the bowl from the body of the
carburetor. Discard the bowl gasket.
You will install a new one.

NOTE

**For convenience, it is better to take
the carburetor off the engine than
to try and make this repair with it
bolted to the engine.**

5. Using an awl or similar tool, press
the float hinge pin from the hinge, remove the pin, and take the float out
of the bowl. The needle valve, which
is attached to the float, will come with
it.

6. Hold the float to your ear and shake it.
If you hear sloshing, the float has sprung
a leak. Get a new float and needle valve
assembly.

7. Press the hinge pin into the hinge and
determine if it fits tightly. If there is any
play between the pin and hinge, get another pin.

8. To guard against the possibility that the
needle valve and seat are worn or damaged, replace both parts.

9. Attach the float and needle valve assembly to the bowl and check to make sure the float is adjusted properly. To do this, place a new gasket around the body of the bowl, and hold the bowl so the float points up. Is the float parallel to the top surface of the bowl—that is, to the surface holding the gasket (Figure 10.2)? If it isn't, use a pair of needle-nose pliers to bend the adjustment tang just a little (Figure 10.3). Check the adjustment again, and follow this procedure until the float and the mounting surface of the bowl are parallel.

10. Reassemble the carburetor and remount it on the engine.

OVERHAULING A CARBURETOR***

The passages inside a carburetor can gum up, especially with machines that have been in use for several years. Closing off the passages will restrict the flow of fuel to the engine and result in hard starting and stalling.

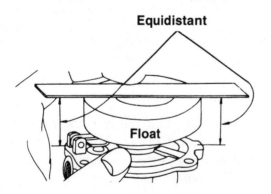

Equidistant

Float

FIGURE 10.2. If the float is adjusted properly, the distance between each of its sides and the rim of the bowl will be the same.

When this happens, you can try to clean and overhaul the carburetor.

A thorough cleaning can be done only by removing the parts of the carburetor. Many of these parts should be replaced. Which ones should be replaced, even if they seem to be in sound condition, and which ones don't have to be replaced has been decided for you by the manufacturer of the equipment who has issued an overhaul (rebuild) kit containing parts. The rebuild kit for your carburetor can be provided by a dealer who carries the particular type of outdoor power machine you possess.

You will probably also need one or more special tools to rebuild a carburetor. There is one tool that allows you to remove the carburetor jet without damaging it. The jet is the part that sprays the fuel mixture into the engine cylinder.

The following guidelines will be helpful as you try to salvage an old carburetor by rebuilding it:

> **CAUTION**
>
> **Wear goggles or safety glasses when doing this job.**

1. Lay out the new parts contained in the rebuild kit. Then, as you remove the carburetor from the engine and take it apart, discard the old parts that are to be replaced by matching them to the new parts.

2. As you take the carburetor apart, make sketches or take Polaroid pictures that will help you to reassemble the unit correctly.

Hinge

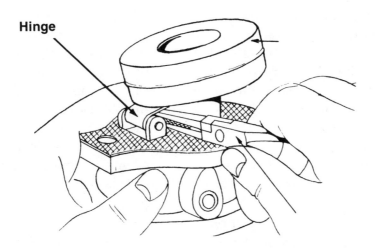

FIGURE 10.3.   To adjust the float, bend the tang under the hinge.

3. Abide by stringent safety and environmental standards as you drain gasoline and remove the carburetor from the fuel tank or engine. Before you begin, be sure to disconnect the cable from the spark plug and point the end of it away from the spark plug terminal.

4. Hold a straightedge across the surface of the carburetor that comes into contact with the fuel tank or engine. Determine if you can slip a 0.002-inch feeler gauge between the straightedge and surface. If you can, the carburetor surface is warped. A warped carburetor surface allows too much air to be mixed into the fuel mixture, which will result in a lean fuel mixture and poor engine performance. You can try to compensate for warpage by using two gaskets when placing the carburetor back on the engine. If doubling the gasket fails to resolve the engine performance problem, you will have to replace the carburetor.

5. If there are nonmetallic parts in your carburetor that are not going to be replaced (because a duplicate part is not included in the rebuild kit), clean them off with a rag and compressed air when you take them out of the carburetor. Then, put them aside. Nonmetallic parts should not be put into carburetor cleaner, which may cause them to erode.

6. Examine the tips of adjustment screws after removing them from the main body of the carburetor. Normally, adjustment screws are not replaced by parts in a rebuild kit. Therefore, if the tip of an adjustment screw does not form a perfectly shaped point, but is bent or worn on a side, buy a new screw.

7. Unscrew the jet from the carburetor and place it in carburetor cleaner for 30 minutes. Then, aim bursts of compressed air into the jet to clear the nozzle. Do not probe the jet with wire.

8. If you are working on a suction carburetor that has a diaphragm, remove the cover over that part. You may or may not have a new diaphragm in the rebuild kit. If you do, discard the old part. If you don't, examine the diaphragm for pinholes and tears. Then, grasp the center disk and attempt to turn the rubber part around the disk. If the diaphragm is damaged, or if it can be rotated around the center disk, buy a new diaphragm.

9. Usually, a new fuel pipe(s) for a suction carburetor will be contained in the rebuild kit. Before you remove an old pipe, determine if it is screwed or pressed into the carburetor.

   If the pipe is screwed into place, you can proceed to remove and replace it without prior preparation. Pipes that are screwed into place have six-sided ends that will accept a wrench (Figure 10.4).

   If you are dealing with a fuel pipe that is pressed into place—it has a round end—measure and make note of the length of the pipe before prying it out of the carburetor. Then, mount the pipe in a vise and pry the pipe off using two screwdrivers, one held on each side of the pipe (Figure 10.5). To install a new pipe and get it the same length as the old one, use a rubber mallet to tap the pipe into the body of the carburetor. Measure the length of the pipe frequently, stopping the procedure when its length equals the length you noted.

10. Before placing the body of the carburetor and metal parts you will be reusing into carburetor cleaner, check the carburetor for small round plugs that are pressed into it. These are called welch plugs and are used to seal passages. To do a thorough job of cleaning the passages, these plugs should be removed. To remove them, sharpen the tip of a small chisel and drive it into a plug. Then, press down and pry up. After cleaning the carburetor, install new welch plugs (available from your outdoor power equipment dealer). Place a

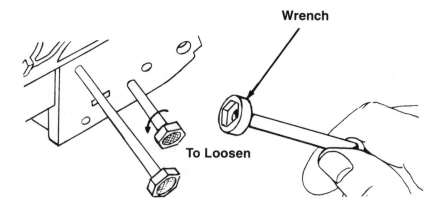

FIGURE 10.4. Fuel feed pipes of suction carburetors that have six-sided ends can be unscrewed with a six-sided wrench.

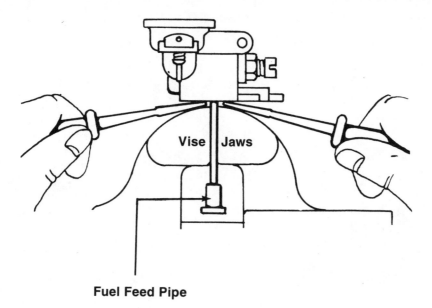

Fuel Feed Pipe

FIGURE 10.5. If the end of the fuel feed pipe of a suction carburetor has a round end, the pipe is pressed into place and can be pried off.

new plug into the hole and use a center punch that is equal in size to the plug to drive the plug into place.

11. Bathe the carburetor body and metal parts in carburetor cleaner for about 30 minutes. Then, use compressed air to blow out passages and dry off the metal. Test the movement of the throttle valve and choke plate to make sure they are free.

12. Reassemble the unit using parts from the rebuild kit.

11

Working on the Starting System

You can start the engine of an outdoor power machine by pulling a rope. There are two variations of this manually operated starter, which is called a rewind or recoil starter:

1. The rope is pulled more or less parallel to the ground. This is a horizontal rewind starter (Figure 11.1).

2. The rope is pulled more or less at a 90-degree angle to the ground. This is a vertical rewind starter (Figure 11.2).

Every outdoor power machine engine has a horizontal or vertical rewind rope starter. When the rope weakens and snaps, you have to install a new rope. It is not a difficult task.

Rope Starter

FIGURE 11.1.   This machine features a horizontal rewind starter.

Some deluxe outdoor power machine models also have a self-starting system that is made up of a storage battery, A/C (for alternating current) generator or rectifier, and an electric starter motor.

When you engage the ignition switch, the storage battery sends a surge of current to the electric starter motor. The starter motor springs into action, and a gear on the end of a shaft emanating from the starter motor is brought into mesh with a gear on the crankshaft. As the starter motor shaft turns, it spins the crankshaft to get the piston in the cylinder to compress the fuel mixture. Simultaneously, the storage battery provides current to the ignition system so the spark plug can fire and ignite the fuel mixture to start the engine. Once the engine starts, the

Rope Starter

FIGURE 11.2.   This machine features a vertical rewind starter.

gear on the end of the starter motor backs away from the gear on the crankshaft. The role of the A/C generator or rectifier is to provide current to recharge the storage battery as the engine is running so the battery will be ready next time it's needed to start the engine.

With a self-starting system, a storage battery can fail to hold the charge needed for the starting process. Furthermore, the terminals of cables connecting the various components can build up corrosion, increasing resistance to the flow of current between components. This, too, will affect the starting process. It is also possible for the A/C generator or rectifier and the starter motor to malfunction.

The remainder of this chapter explains how to replace the ropes of the various types of rewind starters and how to service a self-starting system.

REPLACING A HORIZONTAL REWIND STARTER ROPE**

NOTE
A reminder that the two ** for this project and the one that follows indicate tasks that can be more easily done if you have some do-it-yourself experience.

When a horizontal rewind starter rope breaks off in your hand, don't discard the handle with the tatter of rope attached to it. Lay it aside (Figure 11.3). Then, jot down the model number of the engine. You need this information to get a length of nylon rope of the correct size for your machine from a dealer who sells your make of outdoor power machine. Once you have it, follow these steps to make the repair:

1. Disconnect the spark plug cable and point it away from the spark plug terminal.

CAUTION
Put on a pair of goggles or safety glasses to prevent a possible eye injury if the rewind starter spring should uncurl and fly off the starter housing.

2. The rope and spring that make up a horizontal recoil starter are inside the engine cover so this part has to be removed. You will probably have to take off some parts before you can release the cover. For example, if the throttle control cable is secured to the cover by a bracket or clip, loosen the bracket or clip to release the cable. If the fuel tank is blocking the cover, drain the tank and take it off.

3. When the engine cover is in your hands, turn it upside down to get at the recoil starter (Figures 11.4 and 11.5).

4. Pull out the end of the broken rope as far as it will go. Press your thumb tightly against the pulley or have an assistant do so to keep the spring wound and the rope wrapped around the pulley.

5. Cut the rope off the pulley (Figures 11.6, 11.7, and 11.8). You can now ease the pulley back to the released position.

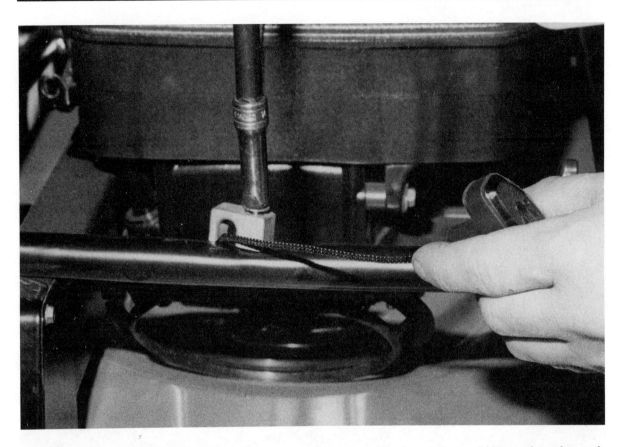

FIGURE 11.3. The handle of the starter rope of many outdoor power machine engines is positioned on the handlebar so the operator can start the engine at this point. You can release the rope by removing the retainer.

6. Before attaching the new rope to the pulley, burn the ends with a match until they get black. Then, cool the ends by pressing a wet cloth against them. Charring the ends of the rope will prevent the strands from unraveling.

CAUTION
Do not hold the match to the rope for too long. The rope could burst into flames.

7. After making sure the ends of the rope are cool enough to handle, make a knot in one end. The knot should fall about $1/8$ inch away from the end of the rope.

8. Wind the pulley counterclockwise until it won't turn any further. Then, back it off two revolutions. Press your thumb against the pulley to keep it from unwinding or, better yet, have an assistant hold it steady so your hands are free to do the work.

137

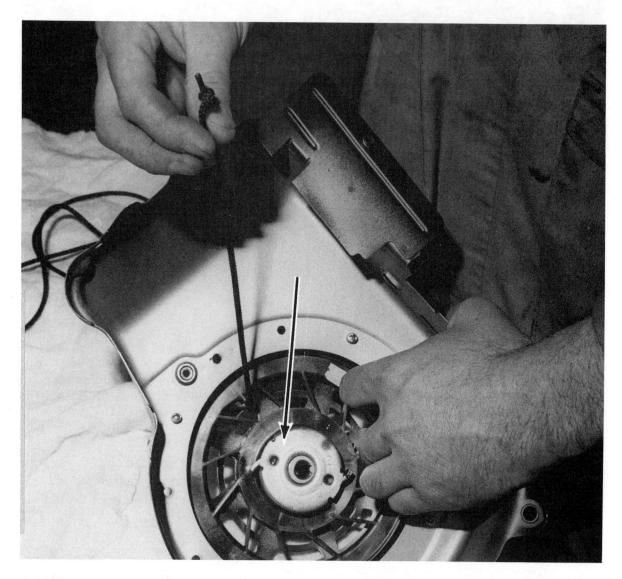

FIGURE 11.4. This recoil starter assembly consists of the rope and an exposed spring (arrow).

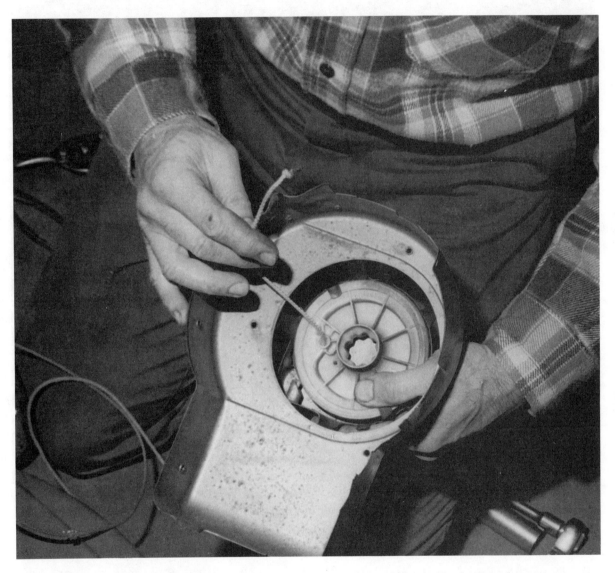

FIGURE 11.5. This recoil starter assembly consists of the rope and a spring that is inside the housing being held by the model.

FIGURE 11.6. Note the metal stress retainer (arrow) on this rope. It is used on machines that have the rope handle held to the handlebar.

9. Thread the new rope through the hole in the pulley (Figure 11.9). Pull out the rope until the knot catches against the pulley.

10. Keep the rope taut as you allow the pulley to unwind. Do this slowly. The rope will wrap itself around the pulley, but stop it when six inches of the rope are still free. Thread those six inches through the hole in the engine cover and make a large knot at this point so this end of the rope will lock itself

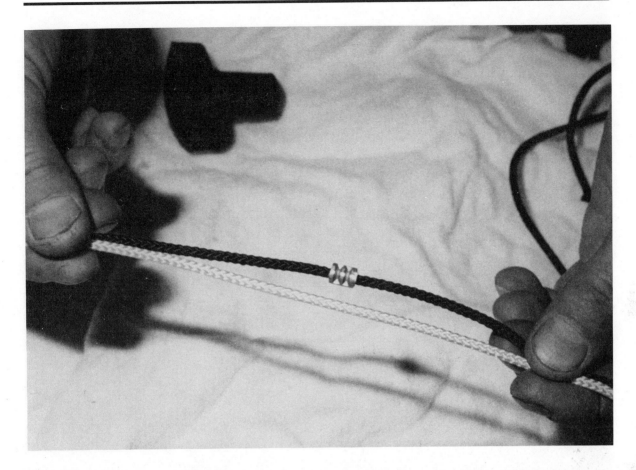

FIGURE 11.7.   After cutting off the old rope, lay out the broken ends of the rope and judge the position of the metal stress retainer that has to be placed in the same relative position on the new rope. Pry off and use the retainer or buy a new one.

against the engine cover and not wrap around the pulley. This is the end to which the handle will be attached.

11. Pry open the end of the handle. Notice that the strand of broken rope still attached to the handle is held by a metal pin or is tied to the handle in some other way (Figures 11.10, 11.11, and 11.12). Make a sketch of how the tatter of rope is held before untying it.

12. Untie the knot you made in the end of the new rope at the engine cover and

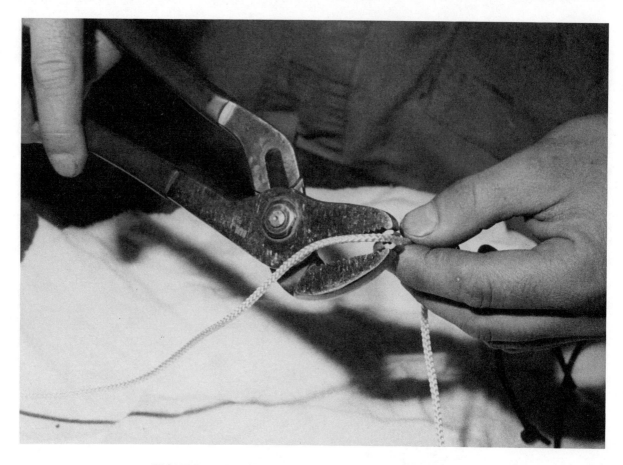

FIGURE 11.8.   Press the retainer on the new rope.

thread that end into the handle. Tie the rope to the handle in the same way that the old rope was held. Then, allow the rope to wind itself fully around the pulley.

13. Bolt the cover to the engine and install the other parts you removed.

REPLACING A VERTICAL REWIND STARTER ROPE**

Start the project by laying aside the handle, purchasing a new rope of the correct length for your engine, and charring both its

---

CAUTION
Put on a pair of goggles or safety glasses to prevent a possible eye injury if the spring should accidentally be released and come flying at you.

---

ends (see previous section). Disconnect the cable from the spark plug and point the end of it away from the spark plug terminal. Unbolt the vertical rewind starter housing from

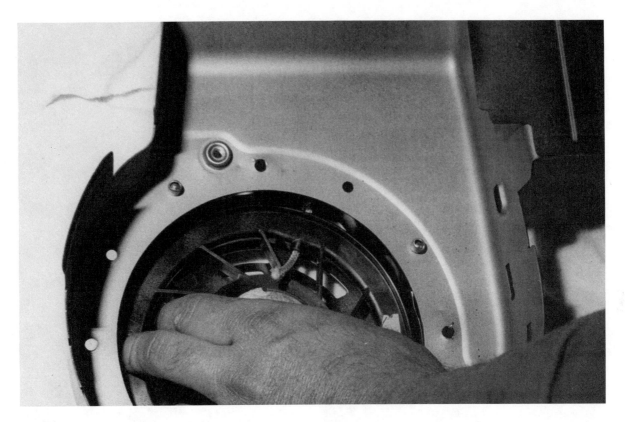

FIGURE 11.9. Pull the new rope through the hole in the pulley until the knot on the other end locks the rope in place.

the engine and examine the mechanism to determine what type of vertical rewind starter you are working with (Figure 11.13). There are two common types:

- The components that control the pulley are under a cover which is bolted to the center of the pulley. The rope is tied to the pulley with a knot that is visible.

- The rope is attached to the pulley by a horseshoe-shaped staple that may not be visible, but which can be brought into view by rotating the pulley.

Here's how to repair both types:

1. If the rope is held to the pulley with a knot, pull the rope out all the way so the pulley is completely wound up. Have an assistant hold the pulley as you cut the rope off the pulley at the knot. The assistant should keep pressure on the pulley until the new rope has been installed.

2. If the rope is held to the pulley with a staple, pull the rope out all the way. Then, let the pulley retract slowly until the staple appears in the notch cut into the pulley housing. Have an assistant hold the

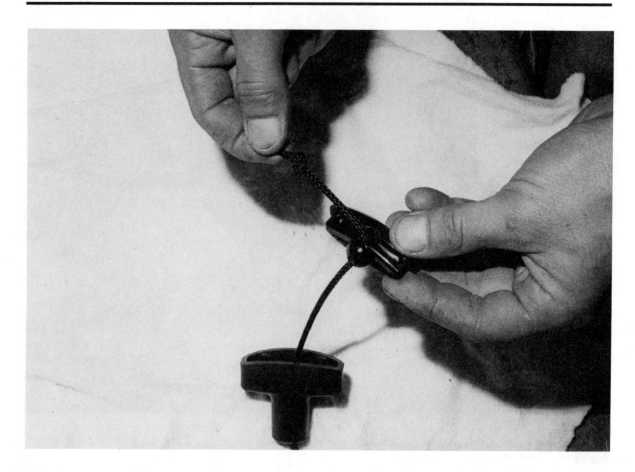

FIGURE 11.10. When you open the end of the handle that still holds the tatter of old rope, you'll see that the rope is retained in the handle by a knot, as here, or by a pin.

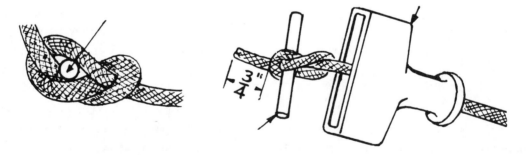

FIGURE 11.11. If a pin holds the rope in the handle, use this illustration as a guide for attaching the pin to the end of the new rope.

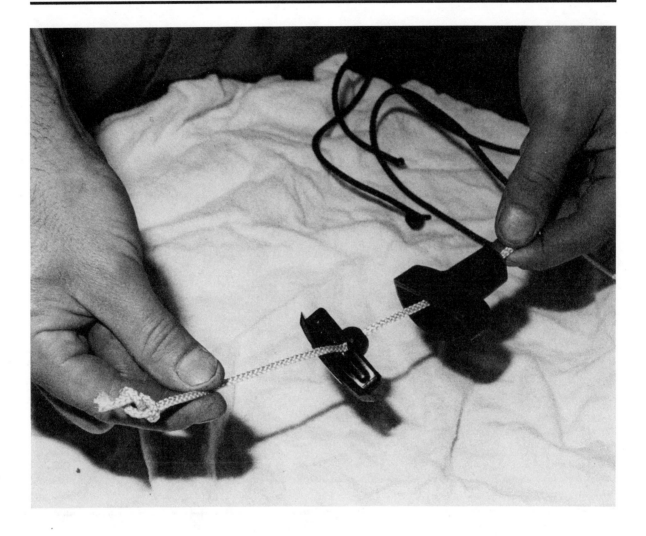

FIGURE 11.12.   If a rope is attached to the handle with a knot, thread the new rope into the handle and tie a knot in the end of it.

pulley in this position as you pry out the staple and release the broken rope. The assistant should keep pressure on the pulley until the new rope has been installed.

3. If the broken rope was held to the pulley with a knot, thread the new rope onto the pulley and tie a tight knot in the end of it so the rope is secured to the pulley.

4. If the original rope was retained with a staple, you do not have to reuse the staple. Just thread the rope onto the pulley and tie a knot in the end of the rope to keep it locked to the pulley. Make sure the knot doesn't rub against the wall of the pulley housing. If it does, trim it with a knife.

FIGURE 11.13. Whether the engine of your machine uses a vertical rewind starter, as here, or a horizontal rewind starter, removing the starter housing is a relatively easy task.

5. With the new rope attached to the pulley, allow the pulley to retract slowly so the rope wraps around the pulley until about six inches of the rope are still left free. Thread this end through the hole in the starter housing, attach the handle (see above), and bolt the starter housing to the engine.

REPAIRING A SELF-START SYSTEM*

The battery and cable terminals of a self-start system are the system's weakest links. If there isn't any response from the starter motor when you try starting the engine, it's a safe bet that one or the other is to blame. Here is what to do:

1. Disconnect cables and use a wire brush to clean the terminals of the cables and the posts of the battery. Make sure that you reconnect the cables tightly to the battery posts and try to start the engine.

NOTE

Remember that the one * given to this project means that it can be done by do-it-yourselfers having little or no experience.

CAUTION

Batteries contain acid, called electrolyte. Wear goggles or safety glasses to protect your eyes. Wear rubber gloves to protect your hands. If acid gets on your skin, wash it off at once. Don't smoke or bring anything that can make a spark near the work area. It might ignite the explosive hydrogen vapors given off by the electrolyte.

---

2. If cleaning the cable terminals and battery posts doesn't resolve the problem, disconnect the cables again, remove the battery from the machine, and take it to a service station to have it tested. If the battery passes the test, have it recharged. If the battery doesn't pass the test, which means there is a dead cell, buy a new battery.

3. Be sure to install the battery correctly. One cable extends from the ground (usually the negative) post of the battery to a ground connection on the engine. The other cable extends from the other post (usually the positive) of the battery to the starter motor.

If a battery passes a test and is recharged, but soon loses the charge again, the cause of the trouble probably lies with the A/C generator or rectifier that is supposed to keep the battery charged. This component should be tested by a technician. If it is defective, it has to be replaced. If the test reveals that the A/C generator or rectifier is not to blame for the starting problem, then the starter motor is at fault. Have a technician determine if this part can be overhauled at a reasonable price. If it can't be, install another starter motor.

12

Overhauling
an Engine

Before discarding an outdoor power machine, because its engine has sustained internal damage, you might want to try your hand at overhauling the powerplant. The cost of the special tools that will be needed is only $20 to $30. Since the project should be done by an experienced do-it-yourselfer, it is given a three *** rating.

Although the engine used in this chapter to describe overhaul is a four-stroke unit, you can follow the same steps if you are working on a two-cycle engine, with one exception: Disregard the procedure involving the oil sump (crankcase) and valves. A two-cycle engine doesn't have an oil sump or valves.

GETTING STARTED

1. Disconnect the spark plug cable and point its end away from the spark plug.

2. Drain gasoline and oil from the engine.

3. Disconnect parts that must be removed from the engine so you can remove the engine from the outdoor power machine —such as covers, drive belt, control cables, and blade.

4. Remove bolts holding the engine to the equipment and take the engine off the equipment.

5. To make it easier to disassemble the engine, place the engine on a stand, which you can get from a dealer who sells your make of engine. You could also make an engine stand from scrap lumber.

6. Remove the spark plug, air cleaner, blower housing, and flywheel screen.

THE DISASSEMBLY PROCEDURE

1. Release the brake-band stop, if one is used, and take off the flywheel (see Chapter 6).

2. Remove the cylinder head and discard the head gasket. You will need a new gasket.

3. If this is a two-cycle engine, remove the bottom cover. If this is a four-stroke engine, remove the bolts holding the oil sump cover and remove the cover. If the cover won't come off, don't pry or bang it with a hammer. Look for a hidden bolt, perhaps under a power take-off cover, which may be bolted to the sump cover.

IMPORTANT

As you remove each part and the hardware that secures the part to the engine, such as washers and nuts, identify the hardware to the part by writing numbers on self-adhering labels or secure the hardware to the part with masking tape. Where several bolts are used to secure a part to the engine, identify which bolt goes into which hole since the sizes of bolts that hold a part often differ. Furthermore, if you think you might have a problem putting something back together again, make a sketch of the assembly or take a Polaroid shot before taking it apart.

4. Clean off the sump cover and unbolt it from the engine.

5. Look inside the sump for a plastic gear. This is an oil slinger. To keep from making a mistake when you put the oil slinger back into the sump, draw a sketch of how it's positioned before lifting it out of the sump.

6. Two gears may now be visible in the underside of the engine. They are the crankshaft and power take-off gears. Rotate the crankshaft slowly until the timing mark on the crankshaft gear is in line with the timing mark on the power take-off gear. Now, lift the power take-off gear out of the sump and retrieve its thrust washer.

7. Loosen and remove the connecting rod cap bolts, and take off the connecting rod cap. If you have trouble getting a wrench on the bolts, rotate the crankshaft until the bolts are accessible.

8. Take the crankshaft out of the engine. To do this, you must first take out the valve tappets. Make sure you identify which tappet goes into which hole. One way to do this is to identify one tappet and its hole with self-adhering labels on which is written "1" and to mark the other tappet and its hole with self-adhering labels on which is written "2." Then, push the piston out of the cylinder and take out the crankshaft.

9. You can now remove the valves.

MAKING REPAIRS

The engine is now disassembled sufficiently so that any damaged parts can be replaced. Inspect the wall of the cylinder for surface scratches. You can bring the engine to a repair shop and have the wall honed to remove this trivial damage. But if there are gouges in the wall, discard the engine.

Examine the crankshaft, connecting rod, piston, and valves. If any part is bent or has sustained other damage, such as erosion of the valve heads and a hole in the piston crown, buy a new part. Be sure to clean carbon from parts that are going to be reused.

REASSEMBLING THE ENGINE

1. If the piston is sound and is going to be reinstalled, be sure to replace the rings around it since piston rings have sustained wear. You will need an expander to get rings off and on the piston.

2. To install the piston, put the piston into a piston compressor that has been lubricated with SAE 20 motor oil. Tighten the compressor until you can barely turn the piston. Then, put the compressor on the engine so the piston is centered over the cylinder. After flooding the compressor and cylinder with oil, push down on the piston. It will slide out of the compressor and into the cylinder.

3. Install all other internal metal parts, but first lubricate them with SAE 20 motor oil.

4. Use a torque wrench to tighten connecting rod cap bolts to the manufacturer's specification, which is given in the repair manual. If you don't have a repair manual, ask the dealer from whom you buy tools and supplies to provide the connecting rod cap bolt specifications. You also need the torque specification for the sump pump bolts, cylinder head bolts, and flywheel nut.

5. Line up the timing marks of the crankshaft and power take-off gears before putting them back together.

6. In putting the oil slinger back in place, make sure that its teeth mesh with the teeth of the power take-off gear.

7. Before installing the sump cover, turn the crankshaft to make sure it rotates freely. If it binds, there is a problem, and you will have to go over what you have done to find it. Protect the crankshaft as you install the sump cover by

placing paper around the shaft. Now if you accidentally hit against the crankshaft with the cover as you lower the cover over the sump, you won't damage the shaft.

8. Be sure to install the flywheel key before mounting the flywheel. Tighten the flywheel nut to the manufacturer's specification.

9. Treat cylinder head bolts with a high-temperature lubricant, such as Never Seize or Lead Plate. Then, using a torque wrench, tighten them using a crisscross pattern.

10. Place the engine back on the equipment and tighten all bolts.

11. Reconnect parts you had to remove to take the engine off the equipment.

PART TWO

Servicing
Two-Cycle Engines

13

How
Two-Cycle Engines Work

Two-cycle (two-stroke) internal combustion engines are used on large outdoor power machines, such as lawn mowers and snow throwers, and on small hand-held outdoor power equipment, such as chain saws and grass trimmers. The two-cycle engine goes through the same four steps in a combustion cycle as a four-cycle engine (see Chapter 1). These steps are (1) intake of fuel, (2) compression of fuel, (3) ignition (or power), and (4) exhaust. However, with a two-stroke engine, the four steps of the combustion cycle are packed into two piston strokes (one up and one down) rather than into four piston strokes as with four-cycle engines.

There is another significant difference between two- and four-cycle engines. There aren't any intake and exhaust valves in a two-stroke engine. Instead, there are a series of passages drilled into the cylinder. Fuel is ingested into the cylinder and waste gases are dispatched through these passages.

THE UP STROKE

As the piston of a two-cycle engine swings up from the bottom of the cylinder after having taken in a charge of fuel, the top (crown) of the piston compresses the fuel mixture, an action that is necessary for the mixture to ignite, burn, and expel energy

(Figure 13.1). At the same time, a vacuum is created in that part of the cylinder vacated by the piston. A fresh charge of fuel is drawn into this part of the cylinder beneath the piston, where the vacuum exists, through a passage leading from an area of high pressure outside the cylinder, which is a carburetor. The passage between these low and high pressure zones is connected by a valve, called a reed valve. The high pressure that exists on the carburetor side of the reed valve pushes the valve into the low pressure zone, thus allowing it to open to let fuel enter the low pressure zone in the cylinder.

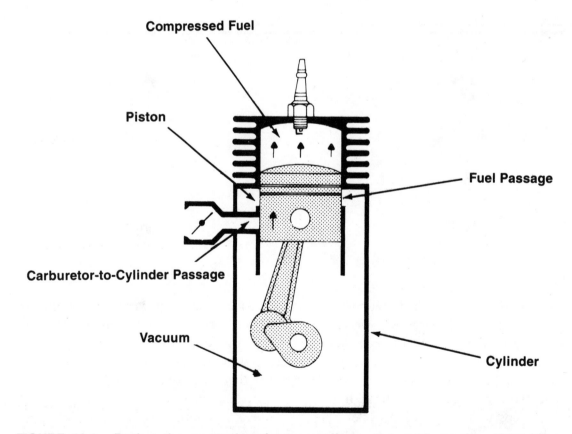

Compressed Fuel

Piston

Fuel Passage

Carburetor-to-Cylinder Passage

Vacuum

Cylinder

FIGURE 13.1. During the up-stroke of a one-cylinder two-cycle engine, the piston compresses the fuel mixture and a vacuum is created in the lower portion of the cylinder.

THE DOWN STROKE

As the piston inside a two-cycle engine reaches the top of the cylinder and starts the down stroke, the pressure under the piston rises to approach the level of the pressure on the carburetor side of the cylinder. Pressure stabilization causes the reed valve to spring shut, which closes off the intake passage so that the flow of fuel into the cylinder is halted. It's at this point that the spark plug fires and ignites the fuel charge, which begins to burn rapidly (almost explosively) (Figure 13.2). The flame spreads from the tip of the spark plug to the walls of the cylinder, producing gases that possess enormous energy which presses against the piston crown to drive the piston down.

As the piston rushes down, it turns the crankshaft by means of a rod that connects the piston and crankshaft. This rod is called the connecting rod. The revolving crankshaft drives the working end of the outdoor power machine, whether it be a blade that cuts grass, paddles that scoop up snow, a stiff piece of nylon string that trims weeds, or chain saw cutters that slice through logs.

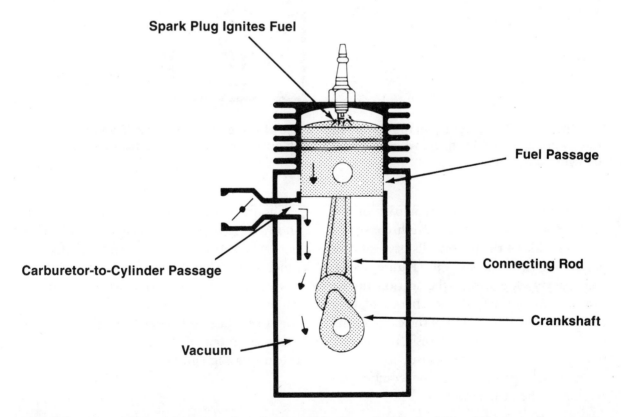

FIGURE 13.2. When the spark plug fires and ignites the fuel mixture, the ensuing energy pushes the piston down, which drives the crankshaft by means of the connecting rod. At the moment that the spark plug fires, the passage from the carburetor to the cylinder is open. This allows a fresh supply of fuel to be drawn into the lower part of the cylinder.

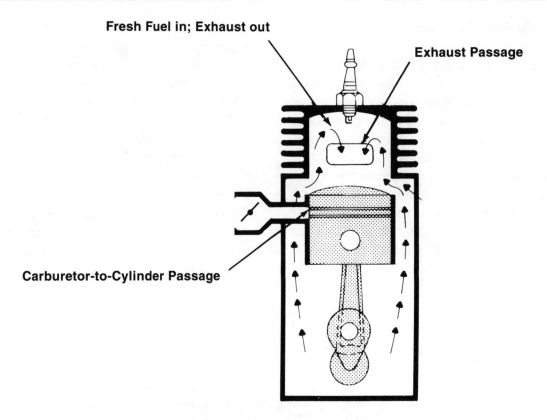

FIGURE 13.3. The next step in the combustion cycle of a one-stroke two-cycle engine as illustrated here is to expel exhaust while drawing a fresh charge of fuel into the combustion area of the cylinder.

As it pushes down into that part of the cylinder which contains the fresh charge of fuel, one side of the piston falls past another passage in the cylinder wall (Figure 13.3). This passage leads from the section of the cylinder where the fresh fuel charge is laying to the combustion section of the cylinder. As the piston plunges into the fresh fuel charge, it displaces the fuel and causes it to flow through the passage into the combustion section of the cylinder.

Simultaneously, the piston falls past still another passage in the cylinder wall. This one, which leads to the outside of the engine, is the exhaust passage. As the new fuel charge rushes into the combustion section, it creates a variance in pressure that helps push the waste gases left over from the previous fuel charge out of the cylinder through the exhaust passage into the air.

14

Maintaining a
Two-Cycle Engine

Maintenance that is performed on a regular basis accomplishes two objectives:

1. It prevents damage that can shorten the life of an engine.
2. It allows engine performance to be maintained at an optimum level.

There are five maintenance procedures which are recommended for two-stroke engines of outdoor power machines. They are:

- Providing the engine with the correct fuel mixture.

- Servicing the air filter.

- Maintaining the correct engine temperature.

- Preparing the engine for a storage period of 30 days or longer.

- Tuning the engine for power and performance.

NOTE

Tasks that have one * can be done by novice do-it-yourselfers. Tasks that have two ** are those that a do-it-yourselfer with some experience should be able to do.

THE FUEL FACTOR*

Unlike four-stroke engines, which run on gasoline that is mixed with air, two-cycle engines require a blend of gasoline and oil that is mixed with air. The oil portion of the blend, which lubricates the walls of the cylinder and sides of the piston as the fuel mixture flows through the cylinder, is burned in the combustion section of the cylinder during the ignition phase of the combustion cycle.

Manufacturers of two-cycle engines claim that the major reason for mechanical failure and poor performance stems from using improperly mixed fuel. You just can't mix gasoline and oil any old way and expect to get sound engine performance or long engine life. Of critical importance are the correct amounts of oil and gasoline which are blended together, the use of the right oil and gasoline, and the mixing procedure itself. Here are the facts you need to know about all of these things:

1. Use 87 or 88 octane unleaded gasoline.
2. Use SAE 30 or SAE 40 oil that is purchased from a dealer of outdoor power equipment. Make sure the container specifies that the contents are for use in two-cycle engines. You should not use oil that is intended for automobile engines.

3. The gasoline must be fresh—not left over and stored. Therefore, buy gasoline the day it is needed. Transport the combustible liquid in a clean, safety-approved container that you can buy from a dealer of automotive parts and supplies. If you purchase too much gasoline, pour the excess into your car's fuel tank.

4. The amounts of gasoline and oil you are mixing must be exactly as specified in the owner's manual. If you have misplaced the owner's manual, write the manufacturer of the equipment for another or ask a dealer who sells the make of equipment for the proper ratio of gasoline to oil.

   The higher number of the ratio refers to the amount of gasoline; the lower number to the amount of oil. Thus, if a ratio of 16:1 is called for, use 16 parts of gasoline to one part of oil. For example, if you are filling a four gallon fuel tank, mix three gallons of gasoline with 24 ounces of two-cycle engine oil.

5. The receptacle that is used to mix gasoline and oil must be scrupulously clean so dirt or water isn't introduced into the engine. To blend the two together, follow these steps:

   - Pour one-quarter of the required amount of gasoline into the mixing container.

   - Add all of the required amount of oil.

   - Screw the cap tightly on the container and shake the container vigorously for at least one minute.

   - Add the remainder of the gasoline.

- Shake the container vigorously for another 30 seconds.
- Insert a clean funnel in the neck of the fuel tank and pour the fuel mixture from the container into the tank.

OTHER MAINTENANCE SERVICES**

A two-cycle engine has either a paper or polyurethane filter to trap airborne dust particles before they can get into the engine. You should open the air filter housing and inspect the filter once a month during the season that the equipment is being used.

Replace a paper filter, if necessary. You can reuse a polyurethane filter after washing and oiling it as described in Chapter 2. Also refer to Chapter 2 for the cylinder head cleaning procedure that will keep temperature at a level below that at which the engine will begin to overheat.

As for putting the engine into storage, the recommendations made in Chapter 2, other than adding oil to the cylinder, should be followed. Substitute the following procedure to protect the cylinder during the storage period:

1. Remove the spark plug and pour two teaspoons of two-cycle engine oil into the cylinder through the spark plug port.
2. Slowly pull the rewind starter rope all the way out and then let it retract slowly to distribute the oil throughout the engine.
3. Reinstall the spark plug.
4. Slowly pull out the rewind starter rope, but this time stop when you feel resistance. Let the rope retract. This places

the sides of the piston over the intake and exhaust passages, which blocks air from entering the cylinder. Air can corrode the cylinder wall.

TUNING UP A TWO-CYCLE ENGINE FOR OPTIMUM PERFORMANCE**

In addition to servicing the air cleaner, insuring proper engine cooling, and servicing the spark plug (see Chapter 3) every 25 hours that a two-cycle engine is operated, tuning the engine for maximum power and optimum performance requires you to clean the exhaust system. The use of oil in the fuel mixture contributes to a significant build up of carbon in the exhaust passage as the mixture burns in the cylinder. If carbon isn't purged from the passage on a regular basis, it will clog the passage. This would create a backpressure in the engine that will cause hard starting and a reduction of power.

Service the exhaust passage as follows:

CAUTION
The engine must be cold.

1. Disconnect the cable from the spark plug and point the end of it away from the spark plug terminal.
2. Unbolt the muffler from the engine to open up the exhaust port (Figure 14.1). Throw away the muffler gasket. You will need a new one.
3. Use a clean wooden implement, such as a popsicle-type stick, to loosen the carbon

FIGURE 14.1.   To service the exhaust passage of a one-cylinder two-cycle engine, start by unbolting the muffler.

in the exhaust passage (Figure 14.2). You can buy these sticks in packages from a store that sells art supplies. As you get near the bottom of the passage, be careful that the stick doesn't slip and hit the piston.

4. Look for a small vent near the exhaust passage and clean that out, too (Figure 14.3). Used in some engines, this vent allows pressure to escape and reduce the effort needed to start the engine.

5. When you have loosened carbon, blow it out of the exhaust passage and vent with compressed air. If you don't have a compressor and air gun, use a can of compressed air that you can buy in a photographic supply store.

6. Inspect the muffler. If it is cracked or bent, get a new one. If the muffler is okay, tap it with a rubber- or plastic-headed mallet to loosen carbon.

7. Attach the muffler to the engine using the new gasket and tighten the bolts (Figure 14.4).

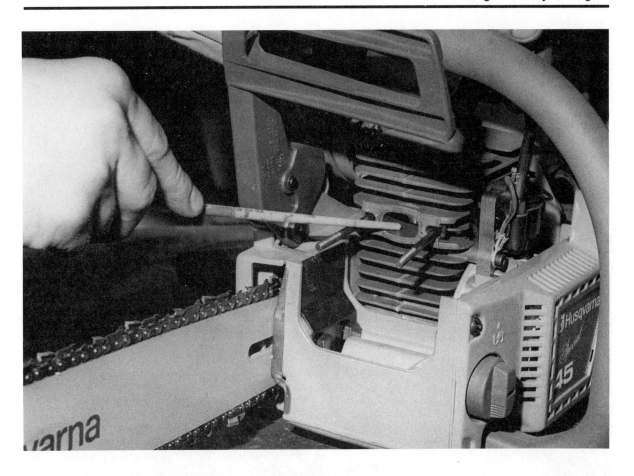

FIGURE 14.2. Use a wooden implement to clean carbon from the exhaust passage.

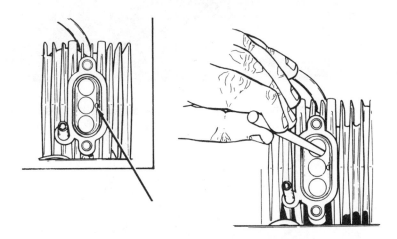

FIGURE 14.3. The exhaust passages of some engines are set up like the one shown in this picture. Note the small vent. It, too, should be cleaned.

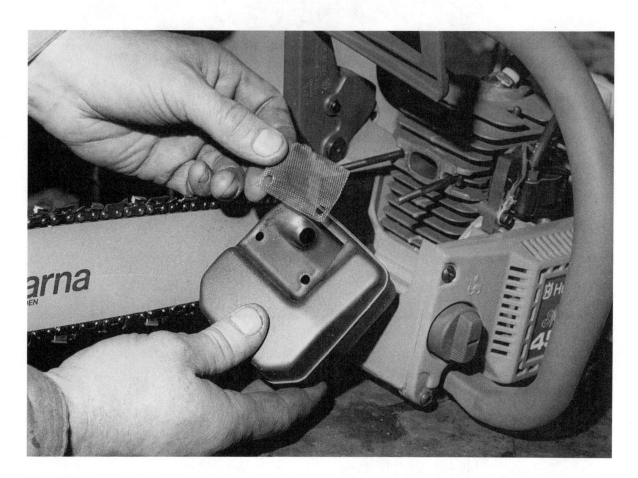

FIGURE 14.4. Mufflers of some one-cylinder two-cycle engines have screens that should be cleaned and reused.

15

Troubleshooting
and Repairing
Two-Cycle Engines

The problems that can disrupt the performance of a two-cycle engine are the same as those that can disrupt the performance of a four-cycle engine. With some slight differences, troubleshooting and repairing these problems are done in the same way, including overhauling the ignition system, carburetor, starting system, and the engine itself. Therefore, if a problem crops up with the two-cycle engine of one of your outdoor power machines, refer to Chapters 6 through 12.

There are, however, three distinctive characteristics applicable to two-cycle engines that come into play in the troubleshooting and repair process. They are the (1) fuel mixture of gasoline and oil, (2) the presence of an exhaust passage that has a tendency to clog because of the carbon produced when the oil-laden fuel mixture burns in the cylinder, and (3) the inclusion of a reed valve in the fuel intake passage between the carburetor and cylinder. Therefore, when a performance flaw with a two-cycle engine crops up, these must be considered along with most of the conditions outlined in Chapters 6 through 12.

PROBLEMS CAUSED BY CHARACTERISTICS SPECIFIC TO TWO-CYCLE ENGINES

An improperly mixed fuel mixture, or one that contains the wrong amounts of gasoline or oil, can make the engine hard to start, miss, lack power, stall, give off an excessive amount of exhaust smoke, or overheat. If one of these problems develops, drain the fuel tank and formulate a fresh mixture of fuel as explained in Chapter 14 to determine if this gets rid of the problem.

Depending upon the degree of an obstruction in the exhaust passage, a two-cycle engine can miss, lack power, stall, or overheat. Therefore, clean the exhaust passage if one of these problems arise (see Chapter 14).

Depending upon the position it is in when it malfunctions, a reed valve that sticks will cause a two-cycle engine to miss, lack power, or stall. The engine might also crank, but not start.

TROUBLESHOOTING A REED VALVE**

NOTE
This note is to remind you that the two ** given to this project indicate that the task can probably be done by someone who has some do-it-yourself experience.

1. Disconnect the cable from the spark plug and point the end of it away from the spark plug terminal.
2. Drain the fuel tank and remove the engine cover, if necessary, to get at the carburetor.
3. Drain the bowl of the carburetor, if necessary.
4. Remove the carburetor from the engine.
5. Remove the bolts that secure the reed valve assembly to the engine, take off the reed valve assembly, and discard the gasket. You will need a new gasket.
6. Examine the strip of tempered steel that is the reed valve. If the valve is bent or cracked, replace the assembly. If the valve doesn't have any visible damage, try to slip a strip of typing paper under the valve. You should not be able to do this. If the paper slides between the reed valve and its seat, replace the assembly.

NOTE
You can't straighten a bent reed valve so there's no reason to try.

PART THREE

Repairing
Outdoor Power Machines
and Electric Power Tools

16

Repairing
Outdoor Power Machines

This chapter discusses the most common nonengine-related maintenance services and repairs that have to be made to snowthrowers, garden tillers, and chain saws. The most common nonengine-related repair that has to be made to a lawn mower—sharpening and balancing the blade—is described in Chapter 8.

The same system of rating projects that has been used throughout this book is continued in this chapter. One * is given to those tasks which novice do-it-yourselfers should be able to do. Two ** are given to those tasks which require some experience.

PREPARING NONENGINE PARTS OF SNOWTHROWERS AND GARDEN TILLERS FOR STORAGE*

Variations in ambient temperature that create condensation, plus dirt left on the equipment, can damage the external parts of a snowthrower or garden tiller that is stored for the off-season. In addition to preparing the engine for storage (see Chapters 2 and 14), the following should be done:

1. Clean the drive chain, if one is used. Then, spray it with silicone lubricant.

2. Lubricate control cables and linkages with the type and grade of lubricant that the manufacturer of the equipment recommends. Also, fill a gear case with the recommended grade of oil. Lubrication requirements are outlined in the owner's manual.

3. Wipe off the snowthrower or tiller auger with a rag. Then, spread a light coating of auto body wax over the part.

4. Cover the inside of a snowthrower discharge chute with a light coating of auto body wax.

5. Wash and dry the machine. To protect its finish during the storage period and help prevent rust, give it a light coating of auto body wax.

REPLACING A DRIVE BELT**

If a drive belt snaps, the snowthrower or garden tiller will stop working. To keep this from happening as you are clearing snow or churning up the earth for your garden, inspect the belt at the start of and once or twice during the season. Look for cracks in the rubber, frayed edges, and a glaze (shine) on the inside of the belt. If any of these conditions exists, install a new belt. Here's how:

1. Disconnect the spark plug cable and point the end of the cable away from the spark plug.

2. Take off the drive belt housing cover.

3. Check the layout of the pulleys (Figure 16.1). There will be two (the rotor and crankshaft pulleys) or three (rotor, crankshaft, and idler pulleys). The crankshaft pulley drives the belt, which turns the rotor pulley that drives the snow-throwing or tilling end of the machine. Machines that have a long drive belt incorporate an idler pulley to support the length of the belt.

4. Disconnect the spring holding the idler pulley. If there isn't any idler pulley, look for a spring on the crankshaft or rotor pulley. If there isn't any spring, look for a screw that is holding the crankshaft or rotor pulley. Disconnect the spring or loosen the screw and remove the belt.

5. Place the new belt on the crankshaft pulley first, and then around the rotor pulley. If you are working with three pulleys, place the belt on the crankshaft pulley and run it under the idler pulley. Then, loop it around the rotor pulley.

    If you find it difficult to get the belt on the rotor pulley, put the edge of the belt on the rim of the pulley. Turn the pulley counterclockwise as you press on the edge of the belt. The belt will fall over the rim of the pulley and into the groove.

6. Make sure the pulleys are aligned properly.

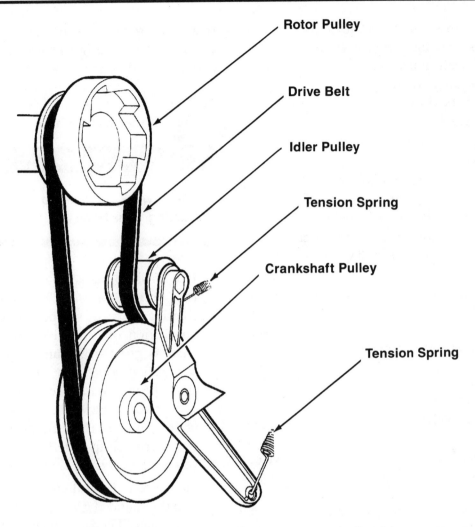

Rotor Pulley

Drive Belt

Idler Pulley

Tension Spring

Crankshaft Pulley

Tension Spring

FIGURE 16.1. **This drawing illustrates the pulley arrangement of outdoor power equipment that uses belts to transfer power from the crankshaft to the working end of the machine.**

ALIGNING DRIVE BELT PULLEYS**

If a belt that drives the working end of your snowthrower or garden tiller jumps off the pulleys, the belt is damaged or the pulleys are out-of-line. Here's what to do:

1. Disconnect the spark plug cable and point the end of the cable away from the spark plug.

2. Remove the belt housing cover.
3. Place a straightedge on the belt to judge whether between the crankshaft and rotor pulleys are in-line. If the straightedge falls at an angle, the pulleys are off-line.
4. Loosen the hex-headed set screw that holds the crankshaft pulley to the crankshaft and slide the pulley on the shaft to get it in line with the rotor pulley. Tighten the set screw.

5. If the machine has an idler pulley, also check the alignment between it and the crankshaft pulley. Since the two are usually right next to one another, this can usually be done by sight, or you can use a straightedge.

6. If the idler pulley is out of line, check to see whether the spring that holds the pulley has detached itself from the pulley. Replace the spring, if necessary, or reattach it. Then, look to see if the idler pulley has an adjustment screw. Loosen the screw and move the pulley until it lines up with the crankshaft pulley. If there isn't any adjustment screw, the idler pulley will be secured to a bracket that can be bent with pliers to move the pulley back into line with the crankshaft pulley.

MAINTENANCE SERVICES FOR CHAIN SAWS*

The nonengine-related maintenance services required to keep a chain saw in condition to prevent damage are described in the owner's manual. They include keeping the oil sump filled with the lubricant recommended by the manufacturer. The oil sump provides lubricant for the chain. You should also keep the machine clean, especially the cooling vents and the holes in the guide bar through which oil is delivered to the chain.

SHARPENING CHAIN SAW CUTTERS**

Each cutter of a chain saw consists of a tooth that does the actual cutting and a raker that sets the depth of the cut. When the waste that is emitted during the cutting operation changes from sawdust to chips of wood, the cutters should be sharpened. Here's how:

1. Tighten the tension adjusting screw to prevent the chain from moving.

CAUTION

Wear work gloves to keep from hurting your hands.

---

2. Use chalk to mark off on the guide bar that section of the chain you will be treating. Confine sharpening to the center section of the guide bar where the chain is given maximum support by the bar. When you finish treating one section of the chain, loosen the tension adjusting screw, move the next section into place, and mark that off. Working in this way keeps you from resharpening cutters you've already sharpened.

3. Place a round metal-cutting file that fits into the rounded grooves of the teeth in a file holder. The file holder keeps the file at the correct angle (usually 35 degrees).

NOTE

The round file and file holder, plus the raker depth gauge and flat metal-cutting file you will need for this operation, can be purchased from a dealer who sells and services chain saws made by the same manufacturer that makes your equipment.

---

4. Place a tooth on the file holder. Then, pressing down on the file, give the tooth a firm stroke, going from the inside of the tooth toward the outside. Release pressure on the file and move the file back to its original position. Then, give the tooth another stroke with the file, and finally a third stroke. Remember that sharpening a tooth is done in one direction only—from the inside of the tooth to the outside.

5. Before going onto the next tooth, set the height of the raker of the tooth you just sharpened. Put the raker depth gauge over the raker and cut the part with the flat file until the top of the raker falls even with the top of the depth gauge. If this causes the front edge of the raker to become square or pointed, use the flat file to round off the edge.

INSTALLING A NEW NOSE SPROCKET**

Your chain saw may have a small gear, called a nose sprocket, on the end of the guide bar. The chain rides on this sprocket. If one of its teeth is damaged, the chain will jump off the guide bar.

Here's how to replace a damaged nose sprocket:

1. Take off the guide bar by removing the nut or nuts that hold it to the body of the tool.

CAUTION
Wear work gloves to keep from hurting your hands.

2. Release the chain from the guide bar.

3. Use a hand drill outfitted with a carborundum grinding wheel to grind off the heads of the rivets that hold the nose sprocket to the guide bar.

4. Drive the headless rivets from place with a punch and hammer. The damaged nose sprocket will fall from place.

5. When you buy a new nose sprocket, notice that the part comes in a plastic case. Don't take the sprocket out of this case. Instead, hold the curved side of the case against the end of the guide bar and slide the new nose sprocket out of the case right onto the bar.

6. Place the rivets that come with the new nose sprocket into the holes of the sprocket and guide bar.

7. Flatten the head of each rivet.

8. Reinstall the chain and attach the guide bar to the saw.

17

Repairing
Electric Power Tools

Power for electric workshop tools comes from a universal electric motor. A universal electric motor converts electric current to mechanical energy. The motor is called universal, because it will run on either alternating household current (AC) or direct household current (DC). Practically all household current in the United States is AC.

The electric drill is a tool that comes to mind when the term "power tool" is mentioned. It has a universal electric motor, but so do other portable (hand-held) tools found in a home workshop, including the circular saw, sabre saw, reciprocating saw, orbital sander, belt sander, and router.

Universal electric motors receive current through cords that are plugged into electric wall outlets, or by a rechargeable battery pack that is contained in a housing that is part of the tool. Stationary power tools, such as drill presses and radial arm saws, are also equipped with universal motors and are therefore no different internally from their hand-held counterparts.

There isn't any difference in the motors of electric home workshop power tools—be they portable with power cords, portable with battery packs, or stationary—except that some are larger than others to provide greater horsepower (Figure 17.1). In other words, all universal electric motors are put together with the same parts and in the same way and suffer from similar problems. You would follow the same procedures for repair as you would if the universal electric motor of any other of your electric power tools failed.

REPLACEABLE PARTS OF POWER TOOLS

The parts of home workshop power tools that fail are the power cord, on-off switch, and the two carbon brushes that are part of

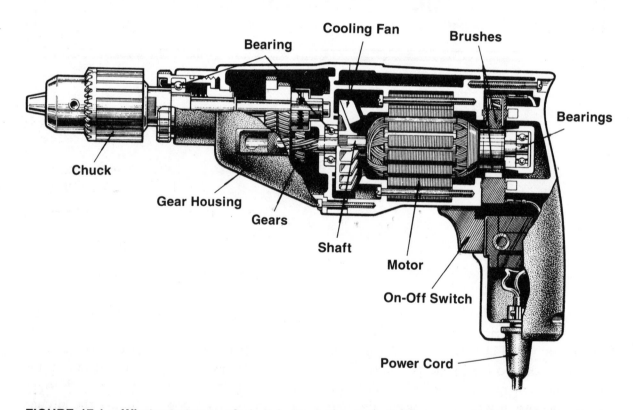

FIGURE 17.1. Whatever types of electric portable and stationary workshop tools you possess, the internal parts are laid out in the same way. Two brushes transfer current to the motor that spins on bearings to drive the working end of the tool, which is a chuck in the case of an electric drill or drill press, through a gear train.

the universal electric motor. It is relatively easy and inexpensive to replace any of these.

When a power cord or on-off switch fails, the power tool won't run. When brushes wear to less than 1/4-inch in length, the universal electric motor may begin to run sluggishly and emit sparks that can be seen by looking into the air vent slots in the sides of the case. If you don't replace the brushes and they continue to wear, the universal electric motor will eventually stop running.

In addition to the brushes, a universal electric motor consists of an armature and stator. The armature, which is also called the rotor, is that part of a universal electric motor that turns the working end of the power tool. It is positioned between the two parts of the stator, which is also called the field coil.

The armature and stator seldom fail, but if one or the other does go bad, the cost of a new part is almost equal to the cost of a new power tool. Therefore, it probably doesn't pay to make the repair.

Throughout the rest of this chapter, which describes how to make the most common repairs, the task rating system that has been used throughout this book is employed. One * indicates a job that a novice do-it-yourselfer can do; two ** refer to a project that a do-it-yourselfer with some experience can tackle.

MAINTAINING ELECTRIC POWER TOOLS*

Maintaining electric power tools helps to prevent damage and is a task that can be done in less than five minutes. After making

sure the cord is disconnected from the electric outlet, do the following:

1. Clean the case with a dry cloth.
2. Inspect the air vent slots. If they are impacted with dirt, wrap a pad of gauze around the tip of a screwdriver and wipe the dirt from the slots. An alternate method is to blow the dirt out of the slots with a can of compressed air that you can purchase from a photographic or computer supply store.
3. To find out if a tool needs to be oiled, examine the case for tiny holes, which are usually marked "oil." The frequency of oiling and the type of oil to use are described in the owner's manual. If you have misplaced the owner's manual, apply two drops of electric motor oil to each hole once every six months.

NOTE

Most power tools are permanently lubricated and do not require oiling.

REPLACING THE CORD AND ON-OFF SWITCH**

Cords of electric tools fail most often because of carelessness. For example, someone may carry a tool by the power cord, allowing the heavy part of the tool to dangle. This puts a strain on the cord and can cause wires to split. Damage will also result if you disconnect the cord from an electric outlet by pulling on the cord. The correct way to unplug a cord is to pull on the plug.

A power cord can also fail because of age. If the insulation hardens and cracks, the motor will still run, but the tool becomes unsafe to use so replace the cord.

An on-off switch can wear out with repeated use. A feeling of looseness as you activate the switch indicates that the switch is going bad.

To replace the cord and/or switch, follow these steps:

1. Disconnect the cord from the electric outlet.

2. Open the case to get at the cord connections and the switch. The case of a power tool is put together in one of two ways. One method is called a clamshell. The other is as a solid casting, but with access to parts.

   If the tool has a clamshell housing, remove the screws that hold the two halves of the housing together and lift one half of the case off the other half. This will reveal cord connections, on-off switch, and motor. If you are dealing with a solid case, gain access to cord connections and the on-off switch by removing the screws that secure the cover over the handle (Figure 17.2). Brushes are reached through holes in the case (see below).

3. Release wires, which are held together by wire nuts or screws, to remove the power cord (Figures 17.3 and 17.4).

4. Examine how wires are attached to the on-off switch (Figures 17.5 and 17.6). If the ends of the wires are inserted into the switch, they are grasped by tangs inside the switch. To release the grip that a tang has on the end of a wire, slide the tip of a thin nail into the hole in which the wire is

---

IMPORTANT

As you disconnect each wire, label that wire and the wire or connection to which it is attached with similar markings. For example, use two self-adhering labels on which you write the same number. Attach one label to one wire and attach the other label to the other wire or to the connecting point. When attaching the new cord or switch, this method will help to insure that you put the parts together correctly. This is important, because reversing connections can result in a short circuit.

inserted, and press down on the tang with the nail as you pull up on the wire. To attach a wire to the switch, reverse the procedure, that is, press down on the tang with the nail, push the wire into the switch, and release the nail. Pull on the wire gently to make sure it is secure.

REPLACING BRUSHES**

You can buy a new set of brushes from a hardware store or a dealer who sells and services power tools. Replace both brushes—not just one. The job is done as follows:

1. Make sure the cord is disconnected from the electric wall outlet.

2. Examine the case for two large caps that have slots in them. They should be

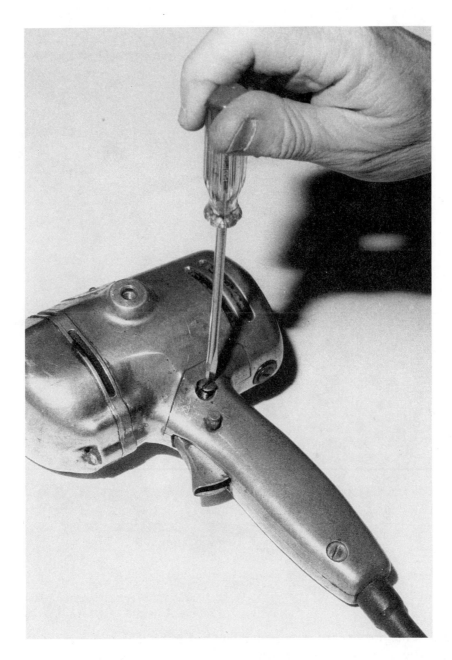

FIGURE 17.2. To replace the power cord and switch of this electric drill, the screws that hold the handle together are removed.

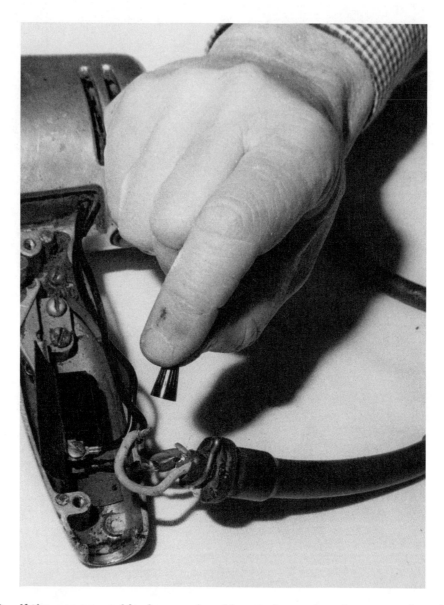

FIGURE 17.3. If the power cord is damaged and has to be replaced, remove the wire nut that attaches the power wires to the motor wire.

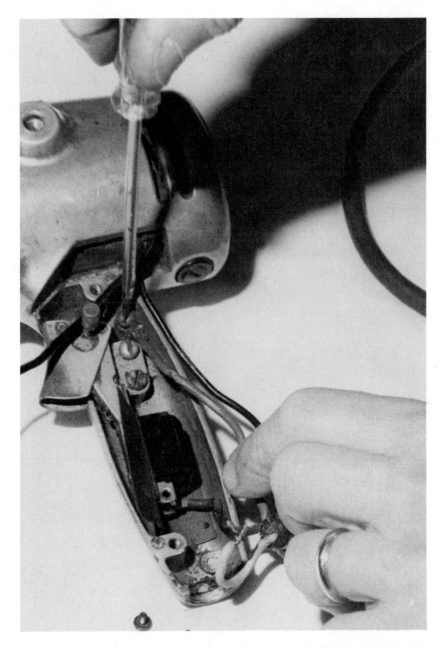

FIGURE 17.4. Then, release the ground wire. It is of utmost importance that you insure that all wires are correctly connected and the ground wire is attached properly when you connect the new power cord. If you aren't sure, do *not* operate the tool.

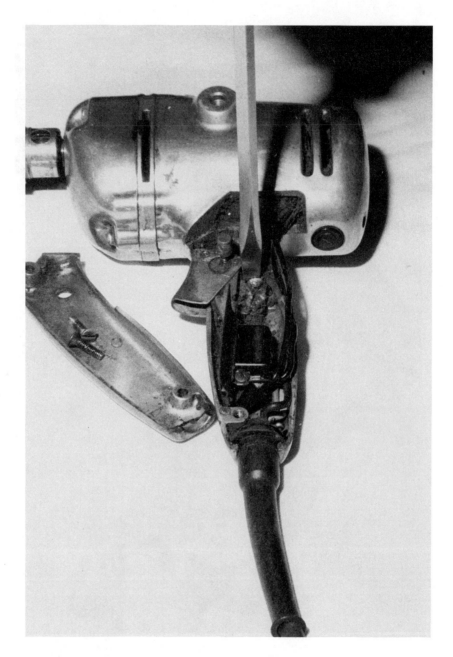

FIGURE 17.5. To replace a bad on-off switch, remove the screws that hold the switch to the case.

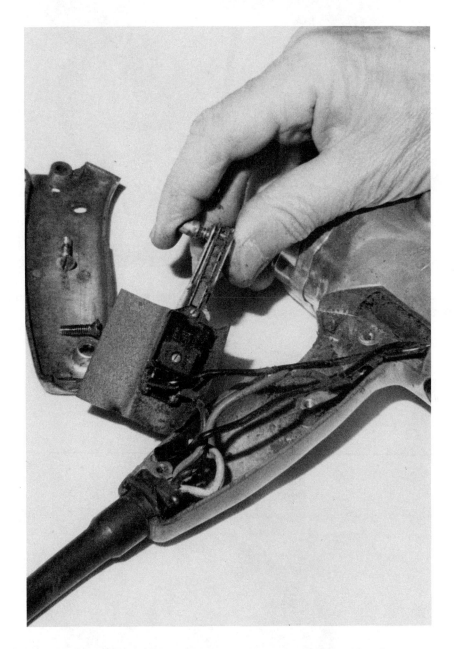

FIGURE 17.6.   Take out the switch and release the wires.

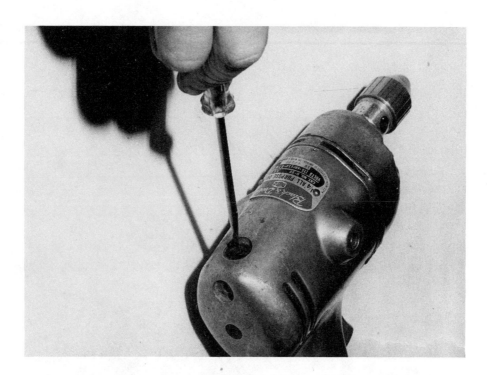

FIGURE 17.7. To replace the brushes, which are the parts of an electric workshop tool that wear out most often, examine the case for brush caps and remove them.

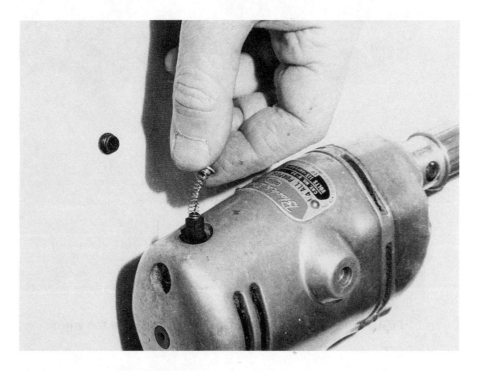

FIGURE 17.8. Remove the old brushes carefully, noticing how they have been installed, and put new brushes into the tool in the same way.

opposite one another. These cover the access holes to the brushes.

3. Use a screwdriver to remove a brush cap (Figure 17.7). Then, slowly draw the brush and spring from the hole. Look to see how the power wire is connected to the brush before you unhook the wire from the brush (Figure 17.8). The wire must be connected to the new brush in the same way.

4. Put new brushes together with springs, attach wires, insert brushes and springs into access holes, and install brush caps.

If you're dealing with a tool that has a clamshell housing and no brush access holes in the case, open the housing by removing the screws. Look for the brushes at the end of the armature. Again, one brush and spring will be directly opposite the other. Examine the arrangement before you release the wires and remove the brushes and springs from their retainers. Insert new brushes and springs in the same way that the brushes and springs you are replacing were retained.

Index